NEEDS ASSESSMENT

NEEDS ASSESSMENT
PHASE I
Getting Started

James W. Altschuld | J. N. Eastmond, Jr.
The Ohio State University   *Utah State University*

Series Editor: James W. Altschuld

NEEDS ASSESSMENT KIT **2**

Los Angeles | London | New Delhi
Singapore | Washington DC

For information:

SAGE Publications, Inc.
2455 Teller Road
Thousand Oaks,
  California 91320
E-mail: order@sagepub.com

SAGE Publications India Pvt. Ltd.
B 1/I 1 Mohan Cooperative
  Industrial Area
Mathura Road, New Delhi 110 044
India

SAGE Publications Ltd.
1 Oliver's Yard
55 City Road
London EC1Y 1SP
United Kingdom

SAGE Publications
  Asia-Pacific Pte. Ltd.
33 Pekin Street #02-01
Far East Square
Singapore 048763

Printed in the United States of America

Library of Congress Cataloging-in-Publication Data

Altschuld, James W.
Needs assessment Phase I: getting started (book 2)/James W. Altschuld, J. N. Eastmond, Jr.
    p. cm.
Includes bibliographical references and index.
ISBN 978-1-4129-7872-9 (pbk.)
    1. Strategic planning. 2. Needs assessment. I. Eastmond, J. Nicholls. II. Title.

HD30.28.A38853 2010
658.4'012—dc22   2009027646

This book is printed on acid-free paper.

09   10   11   12   13   10   9   8   7   6   5   4   3   2   1

Acquisitions Editor:	Vicki Knight
Associate Editor:	Lauren Habib
Editorial Assistant:	Ashley Dodd
Production Editor:	Brittany Bauhaus
Copy Editor:	Melinda Masson
Typesetter:	C&M Digitals (P) Ltd.
Proofreader:	Victoria Reed-Castro
Indexer:	Diggs Publications Services, Inc.
Cover Designer:	Candice Harman
Marketing Manager:	Stephanie Adams

Brief Contents

Detailed Contents

Preface

Anyone who has done any type of study knows that starting the endeavor is almost always the most difficult part of the process. Going further it is often harder to think about questions and finding answers to them than it is to actually do the investigation. This is equally true of needs assessments, especially as they are conducted by organizations.

What kinds of thinking occur in organizations, agencies, and businesses that eventually lead to doing assessments? How do they start, and what activities should facilitators and needs assessment committees (NACs) be implementing to get the endeavor off the ground in a positive manner? While there is now a fair amount of literature on needs and their assessment, there is far less about how such an important activity begins and what actions enhance the promise of a fruitful outcome.

To that end, this book in the KIT deals with Phase I (preassessment) of needs assessment. What about the organizational culture and the likelihood of key decision makers being willing to shift their energies to focus on new problems and ways of operating? How open or closed is the organization? What are some relatively easy mechanisms for collecting existing data and for utilizing the skills and experiences of the individuals on the NAC to do so? If there are many potential need areas, how should the committee decide which ones to pursue? How should members sort through things? How might politics and local conditions affect what should be done? What values are there, and what role might they play?

We have provided procedures and activities that could be done in this phase. The underlying goal, once the dynamics of the setting are understood, is to rely as much as possible on information in reports, data archives, and the like. By utilizing what is available, a lot can be learned without the costs and efforts associated with getting new data. The assumption is that much information is there and ripe for the picking;

don't initiate anything until you know what is accessible and what it tells you. Tied into this thinking is a corollary that if organizations are rich in information that circumstance may by itself afford a reasonable look at needs and offer enough insight for making decisions about them. Only when there is insufficient information is it necessary to move to Phase II and expend the resources necessary for additional data collection.

❖ A NOTE ABOUT USING THE TEXT

Needs assessment is not an exact science with rules and structures that have to be followed to the letter. Every situation and context is different, and techniques will have to be adopted to fit such realities. Numerous forms, procedures, and ideas are included in the text as illustrations of what might be done but with the recognition that local imagination and ingenuity will affect how they are perceived and used. Adapt them to be more applicable to the specific assessment being undertaken and consider publishing these adaptations to enhance the work of needs assessors in other venues.

As indicated in its title this is Book 2 in the Needs Assessment KIT. The others are:

Book 1: *Needs Assessment: An Overview*

Book 3: *Needs Assessment Phase II: Collecting Data*

Book 4: *Needs Assessment: Analysis and Prioritization*

Book 5: *Needs Assessment Phase III: Taking Action for Change*

Reference, when appropriate, will be made to other books in the KIT. If you need more ideas on how to implement an assessment you are encouraged to consult them.

Acknowledgments

It is obvious and openly admitted that the content of the book comes heavily from our long experience and work in conducting assessments. We express gratitude to those individuals who joined us on these journeys and enhanced our thinking about assessment via their input and recommendations. Two of the most influential of these are Jefferson N. Eastmond and Belle Ruth Witkin, both deceased. Without the input of all our fellow needs assessors, the text would have been far less rich and thoughtful. Beyond that, many of the sponsors of the studies of needs were willing to allow us to experiment with the strategies employed, even to the point of doing research within the confines of the assessment. Thank you so much for your openness and support of ways to improve the quality of what we have done.

Last, we extend our deepest appreciation and love to our families in Ohio and Utah, respectively. Thank you always for all of the things (large and small) that you have done and continue to do to pave the way for our efforts. Without you everything pales in significance.

The authors and SAGE gratefully acknowledge the contributions of the following reviewers:

Stephanie Brzuzy, *Xavier University*

Melanie Otis, *University of Kentucky*

Kui-Hee Song, *California State University, Chico*

—James W. Altschuld
—J. N. Eastmond, Jr.

About the Authors

James W. Altschuld, PhD, received his bachelor's and master's degrees in chemistry from Case Western Reserve University and The Ohio State University (OSU), respectively. His doctorate is from the latter institution with an emphasis on educational research and development and sociological methods. He is now professor emeritus in the College of Education and Human Ecology at OSU after 27 years of teaching research techniques and program evaluation. In evaluation, he developed and taught a sequence of courses on theory, needs assessment, and design. He has coauthored three previous books (two on needs assessment and the other on the evaluation of science and technology education), has written many chapters on needs assessment as well as others on evaluation research and issues, and has an extensive list of publications, almost all in the field of evaluation. He has given presentations and done work in five countries outside of the United States. In his career he has been the recipient of local, state, and national honors including the Alva and Gunnar Myrdal Practice Award from the American Evaluation Association for contributions to evaluation.

J. N. Eastmond, Jr., PhD, received his bachelor's degree in economics from the University of Utah, his master's in elementary education from Ohio University, and his doctorate in educational psychology from the University of Utah. Currently, he is professor of instructional technology at Utah State University. He has published extensively in journals and has numerous book chapters on ethics, needs assessment, and technology.

1

Overview

❖ WHY A WHOLE BOOK DEVOTED TO
GETTING A NEEDS ASSESSMENT GOING?

Each of us has spent more than 30 years working on needs assessment
and related topics, and we have seen our share of failures. Some investigations have been too broad and others too narrow, resulting in their
needs-based findings not being used and having limited impact on organizational behavior and policies. Organizations asking for assistance
with a needs assessment may not understand what the term connotes,
what the process of assessment might entail, that there are many different types of needs (maintenance, short and long term, and service recipient/
provider), and so forth. At times, needs assessment is confused with
evaluation of programs in regard to implementation and outcomes.

Given our collective observations, the obvious concern is helping
schools, businesses, institutions, health organizations, and others
obtain a meaningful perspective on needs and how to assess them. The
problem is compounded in several additional ways. First, typically
needs assessments are guided by an external consultant or facilitator
who does not have intimate knowledge of the organization, the constituencies it serves, and most important, how it makes decisions. Even
when internal assistance is provided, the facilitator is an outsider

1

brought in to do a job and probably is not involved when needs are translated into action plans for either changed or new activities of the organization.

Second, published reports of assessments seem to focus more on the methods employed and the final results and less on the deliberations leading to beginning the activity. Internal reports are not so easily accessed since they were for organizational rather than publication purposes. And, if accessible, it is likely that they will be similar to published reports—long on methods and findings and short on what initially happened as the organization decided to do an assessment and the subtle nature of those early discussions and considerations. The topic isn't omitted; it's just not given much play in the scheme of things.

Third, whether a study of needs is or is not successful, evaluations of the process and what results from it are not noticeable in the literature. The resources and time devoted to examining needs may deplete the psychic energy required for evaluation, or there simply is little interest in doing so. (See Stevahn & King, 2010, Book 5 in the Needs Assessment KIT, for utilitarian procedures for evaluating assessments.) Whatever the case may be, there is not extensive documentation of what goes on early in the game of assessing needs. That part of the process is murky.

Lastly, other problems come to the fore that must be attended to as the assessment gets underway. Such things as forming a needs assessment committee (NAC) to oversee the effort (not done nearly as frequently as it should be), employing strategies to guide this group and enhance its effectiveness and efficiency, gaining a better sense of the organization and how it works through cultural audits and microethnography, thinking through the possibility of a collaborative assessment across institutions for the assessment and the eventual resolutions of underlying problems shared by them, attending to the subtle but ever so necessary communications about the process to staff and decision makers, and other activities all have problematic dimensions to them.

For reasons like these it seems imperative to offer suggestions and direction for getting the assessment off on a positive note—one that leads to higher likelihood of information being used for decisions and organizational improvement. This is the rationale for this book. It emanates from many situations we have seen or been engaged in or from what we have found in the literature. It includes examples of what has been done to get the assessment going.

In Table 1.1, an overview of the three phases of needs assessment is given with steps for each phase. The bolded entries in the first row are the focus of this book.

Table 1.1   The Needs Assessment Model (Phases and Key Steps)

Phase	Overarching Phase Descriptor	Key Steps
Phase I Preassessment	**Focusing the needs assessment, and what do we know about possible needs?**	1. **Focusing the needs assessment** 2. **Forming an NAC** 3. **Learning as much as we can about preliminary "what should be" and "what is" conditions from available data sources** 4. **Moving to Phases II and/or III or stopping**
Phase II Assessment	Do we need to know more, will we have to conduct a much more intensive data collection effort, and do we have ideas about what are the causes of needs?	5. Conducting a full assessment about "what should be" and "what is" conditions 6. Identifying discrepancies (Levels 1, 2, and 3) 7. Prioritizing discrepancies 8. Causally analyzing needs 9. Preliminary identification of solution criteria and possible solution strategies 10. Moving to Phase III
Phase III Postassessment	Are we ready to take action, and have we learned enough about the need to feel comfortable with our proposed actions?	11. Making final decisions to resolve needs and selecting solution strategies 12. Developing action plans for solution strategies, communicating plans, and building bases of support 13. Implementing and monitoring plans 14. Evaluating the overall needs assessment endeavor (document with an eye to revisit and reuse)

Source: From *Needs Assessment: An Overview,* by J. W. Altschuld and D. D. Kumar, 2010, Thousand Oaks, CA: Sage. Used with permission.

❖ HOW DOES A NEEDS ASSESSMENT START?

How does one begin thinking about needs assessment? What ought to be asked up front? How do we know if such a study is necessary? What are the indications if it is not? Will conducting an assessment change the climate of the organization? How do we know that it is worth doing? We hope to provide some answers to these questions and a few more besides.

Getting launched on an assessment effort may seem to involve some sleight of hand, with parts of it quite evident and others hidden beneath the surface. For anyone getting into it, there is a mixture of instinct and thoughtful action, of heuristics for problem solving and intuition regarding the best ways to go.

❖ CONCERNS, TOP-DOWN OR BOTTOM-UP?

As people speak to you about the organization, they often express "areas of concern." These are valuable clues that lead to uncovering real needs; however, the fact that someone expresses a strong opinion does not mean that there will always be a real need there. Having a concern simply implies that some aspect of the organization possibly could use a reexamination, some reflection, or a remake. Engaging in an assessment will provide some answers as to which of these deserve closer attention or are not worth pursuing.

The issues or concerns can come from the top of the organization, possibly from a CEO (chief executive officer) who feels change is needed for the continued survival of the organization or to make current operations more effective. In these cases, there will frequently be "buy in" from administrators but perhaps little awareness or support for the idea from the rank and file.

Conversely, there may be a groundswell of opinion coming from within the organization that something has to be done. Individuals working for a company in the U.S. automobile industry in the early 21st century are acutely attuned to the fact that hybrid cars are making huge profits for their competition. As an outgrowth of this, they might push for some kind of organizational redirection that would help them maintain their jobs and lifestyle in the years ahead. (Having Detroit's Big Three automakers go hat in hand to Washington has underlined the obvious: Detroit must change how it builds cars and the kinds of cars it offers to become more profitable.) Assessments can start out like that—where there is enough indication that new endeavors are necessary, the rank and file of the organization begin to agitate for change.

❖ AN INVITATION TO SYSTEMATIC PLANNING

Systematic planning, as opposed to just reacting, is the preferred mode for dealing with a small or a large problem. Instead of acting hastily based on a personal hunch, systematic planning is reflective and careful, taking decision making through step-by-step procedures that eventually result in more clearly delineated problems and better solution strategies. Data-based decision making turns out, in most instances, to be superior to intuition, although it requires more effort. The energy expended on contacting reality, through experience and empirical data, pays off in the short and the long run.

The habit of distinguishing needs from solutions is one of the best mental skills that a would-be needs assessor can cultivate. As an introduction to assessment thinking, a common exercise is to ask a group to make a list of what its members perceive to be needs. To a group of school people, the resulting list might contain better facilities and teachers, higher salaries, more computers, and the like. Then, midway through the process, the facilitator interjects: "But most of these are all solutions, not needs." And the group then backs up, while the facilitator explains: "The primary need at the learner level is that students in your school lack the skills in thinking—or reading, writing, and arithmetic—that society will require of them to be successful contributing members. Having more computers (or better-trained teachers in nicer buildings) is a way of resolving that need." Group members are then coached on the definition of a need, a gap between what is and what should be, and to stay watchful for solutions masquerading as needs.

This type of thinking applies to all fields. Another example would be in health, where some institutions first consider the needs of patients (Level 1 or service recipients) before redesigning the focus and structure of hospital rooms. Instead of having to change rooms, patients stay in the same room, to the extent possible, with services coming to them. This arrangement creates a more stable, less threatening environment in what is a stressful time for an individual.

Keeping the two concepts (need and solution) separate takes a focus that is required for real "problem identification" and "problem definition." This distinction of the difference between needs and solutions is an essential premise of systematic planning and guides us in selecting key problems for solution. (See Book 1 of the KIT for other ways to get a group thinking about needs.)

As we work on Phase I of the needs assessment process, it is important to keep in mind that eventually one of three decisions will be made (see Step 4 in Table 1.1):

1. The need identified is not significant enough to take action. The effort can STOP THERE, because no further action is warranted.

2. The need is there, enough to justify doing a full study, and it will require A FULL EFFORT to carry it out.

3. The need is there, but WE KNOW ENOUGH NOW TO PROCEED to action planning for resolving it.

At the end of this chapter, these three decision points will be revisited.

❖ SOME PRELIMINARY THOUGHTS ON GETTING THE NEEDS ASSESSMENT UNDERWAY

Consider the steps required to get a needs assessment underway since successful ones do not just happen. They require careful homework, thoughtful negotiation, institutional buy-in, and then skillful conduct and follow-through. The process is something that you can engage in and do well. Many people have learned how to intuitively complete such an investigation on their own. Hopefully, our ideas will enhance the work of individuals with experience and provide concrete direction for those who are just entering into the activity. What follows are the important steps in getting the process started, beginning with important preconditions:

1. Careful homework

To some extent, the homework for "coming up to speed" will depend upon your role in the process and whether you are an internal employee of the organization or an external consultant engaged to facilitate the assessment. In either case, here are some questions you should be prepared to answer, with a short and not particularly detailed response, prior to undertaking an investigation of needs:

- What are the major goals and mission of the organization as seen from inside and from outside perspectives?
- Who are the clients and organizations that hold this group accountable?
- What issues or controversies has the organization had to face recently, and what are the existing impacts (and/or scars)?
- What kinds of behavior does it take to succeed as an employee of the organization? What kinds of actions would be seen as "off limits"?

In the beginning it is necessary to have a sense of these questions and to realize that some behind-the-scenes effort will almost always be required.

2. Thoughtful negotiation

The "p" word (*politics*) often raises its head in needs assessment. The outcomes of such a study are intended to impact the direction of the organization, so why wouldn't people be expected to work to influence them? In every assessment, the person charged with conducting it must enter into negotiations with key people, to determine (a) the way the study will be done including constraints that might be entailed in doing it; (b) the level of resources, money, and people's time to be made available; (c) the question of whom from the organization will be participating in it; and (d) the expectations held by those in leadership positions to take action on the results.

To the facilitator, some parts of the negotiations should be considered desirable but expendable if push comes to shove, while others would be nonnegotiable, to be held onto at all costs. The stance that you take and how strong it is depend quite a bit on whether you are internal or external to the organization. In Table 1.2, some of the factors in negotiation have been sorted along the line of what was just described.

Table 1.2   Some Negotiables and Nonnegotiables in Needs Assessment

Negotiables	Nonnegotiables
Time allowable to complete the study (with some flexibility)	Editorial control of the written reports
Level of resource support	Commitment to democratic involvement of all stakeholders
Personnel time (especially the NAC)	
Secretarial/data handling expertise	Means of conducting and reporting fit within ethical guidelines for research, including Institutional Review Board (IRB) requirements
Funding for persons involved	
Access to various data sources	

(Continued)

Table 1.2 (Continued)

Negotiables	Nonnegotiables
Ways that information will be made public	
Awareness within all levels of the organization for which a study is being conducted	Institutional commitment to see the study through to completion
Opportunity to present findings verbally	Diverse representation on the NAC

In negotiating, know your position but be as flexible as you can be, within some preestablished limits. To use an example from Mauritius (a long-term island stay for one of the authors), just as it is to the advantage of a taxi driver or a fruit vendor to negotiate price from a position of strength, knowing full well the acceptable limits of negotiation, so it helps the needs assessor to have thought through a personal position on these items. While some issues may be left "under the table" and not discussed, it still is important to have considered such things.

Why are editorial control, commitment to complete the process, commitment to democratic involvement, representation of diversity, and an ethical basis for operation nonnegotiable? With each of these, the integrity of the facilitator and assessment process is at stake. If you compromise on these elements, the credibility of the effort could and undoubtedly would come into question. By the same token, there has to be some give and, when negotiating, be strong but with the understanding that accommodations are possible and can be made.

Why are the other factors negotiable? They have more wiggle room within acceptable practice. If the resources available are limited, the resulting product will show those limitations. Of course, there is a baseline level, and if not there, it would be best to withdraw from conducting the study, as noted in Book 1.

❖ INSTITUTIONAL BUY-IN

Before seriously embarking on a needs assessment, it is imperative that the organization involved give its formal support to the activities to be completed and the decisions to be made; otherwise, a host of barriers may surface to smother the assessment. "Why are you planning to ask these people questions like these?" and "Why do you need access to these files?" are resolved if the institution has "bought in" and approved the assessment but almost impossible if it has not.

How does one know if there is legitimate buy-in? The word *buy-in* connotes a monetary transaction and that provides a clue to an answer. When the needs assessor puts into writing a formal proposal, and when important decision makers approve it, including the provision of resources for looking at needs, one can be certain that the institution has given formal approval and "bought in."

When involvement is more informal, as in the case of a one afternoon assessment of recreation needs for retirees in a senior citizen housing center, the commitment is less formal but no less important. In this case, the agreement could have been cemented by a vote of the management committee of the seniors and/or a handshake with the center director. Until you have this official "buy-in," you would be wise not to proceed beyond some basic fact-finding.

The value of a written contract or a memorandum of agreement is worth stressing. This document clarifies the expectations on both sides and reminds the assessor and the organization of the extent of the effort. Eastmond, Witkin, and Burnham (1987) argued that a contractual arrangement is one of the best ways to prevent growing expectations from overwhelming the resources of those charged with conducting the study. Also observe that a written contractual arrangement is listed as one of the elements of Propriety in the Joint Committee Standards for Evaluation (1994) and is encouraged by several entries in the American Evaluation Association's (2009) *Guiding Principles for Evaluators*. With few exceptions, having a written document is good practice. This is true even though it may not be possible to specify all the fine details at the beginning of the needs assessment.

❖ SKILLFUL CONDUCT AND
FOLLOW-THROUGH OF THE NEEDS ASSESSMENT

Having an experienced and capable facilitator is critical for this type of work. In fact, every assessment requires some fine tuning in regard to leadership, the level of expertise of the persons involved from the organizational side, and particularly the membership of the NAC. Needs assessments are learning experiences, and the individuals and the organization benefit from mistakes as well as from successes.

Next consider resources as a full assessment can require much time, money, personnel, angst, and so forth. To use a parallel, it is not wise to undertake the building of a house until all the needed materials and skills are in hand. It is better to hold off on conducting an assessment until adequate resources and energy can be mustered to do the job completely. Because what is available is often insufficient, the constant mantra will be on creative ways to extend what you have by delegating tasks or completing joint projects with other agencies and thus sharing the load. But a detailed and close look at what will be required to complete the study of needs is extremely important. And there is no more advantageous time to determine such requirements than "up front," before the whole shebang begins.

❖ THE THREE DECISIONS REVISITED

For a moment, examine the three phases of needs assessment and the steps imbedded in them (see Table 1.1). The whole procedure is dependent on what happens in Phase I with virtually all other activities coming from what is done early in the game. The results of initial efforts lead to three possible decisions to be made. They are important, and two of them will entail additional support from the organization. Phase I is absolutely critical for needs assessment.

Option 1: The need identified is not significant enough to take action

The effort can STOP THERE, because nothing further is warranted.

This is a very common outcome, since seldom are detailed and comprehensive assessments found in the literature. Many times from the viewpoint of an organization and the wherewithal it has, the justification for conducting a total effort simply does not surface. Instead, small assessments and on-course corrections are more frequently observed.

There is nothing wrong with this position, unless there is a significant reason for taking a closer look at needs. There may be external pressure, as from an accrediting agency or oversight authority, to show that a thorough needs assessment has been done. Unfortunately, if the process is instigated in response to such a press, it may not have the commitment of the group to follow through once that press is gone (e.g., when the accreditation visit is over). Care must be exercised to ensure either (a) that the people inside the organization are convinced that the needs assessment is for a good purpose or (b) if stopping is justified, that that decision be made deliberately and not lightly. If the latter course is chosen, it can save resources and wear and tear on the nerves and patience of staff members, and it may be the propitious way to go. Needs assessments don't always have to be undertaken!

Option 2: The need is there and warrants going to Phase II

Making the commitment to undertake a full assessment is a serious matter—it not only will use resources but may also bring the values (even conflicting ones) of the organization into sharp focus. That being said, it is notable that the uncovering of facts and values can build an important base of information for an organization. The capacity of the organization is strengthened as key people reexamine their core values and eventually arrive at a group stance about them. Those served by the organization, Level 1 constituents, in this instance could be flattered if information had been collected from them and that someone would come to them and ask their opinions about important needs. At times basic assumptions regarding Level 1 are simply taken for granted (and overlooked) in the day-to-day operation of an enterprise.

Option 3: The need is there, but we know enough now to proceed to carry out an action plan

This option might be appealing, because it leads to action and saves resources and effort that would be involved in an extensive study. The feeling to get right on with the business at hand is tangible. But so too is the possibility that we could be going ahead with false or incomplete information to everyone's detriment. Our advice to those wanting to take this step is to ask some questions:

- What are the needs being addressed? Are they clearly spelled out for others to see?

- Are the actions proposed grounded in these basic needs?

- How confident are you that these are coming from actual data and the experience of people in the situation?

- Have you heard these needs expressed from a variety of constituents (important stakeholders)? Can you say that the sentiments represent enough of a broad cross section that there will be confidence in the results (you won't be blindsided by opposition or challenge from someone from a different part of the organization)? If answers are favorable for moving along, do so, knowing that you are saving resources that can now be devoted to action planning.

❖ ONE ADDITIONAL FEATURE

As a way of making the text more concrete, an example of one recent needs assessment for a university department of instructional technology will be given in the remaining chapters. While not without flaws it illuminates decisions made early in the needs assessment process. The impetus for the study was mainly external, accreditation for the department. Additionally there was urgency for the study due to (a) the loss in one year of 4 of 10 faculty members, some of whom had national reputations; (b) department hopes to stay among the five top-ranked programs in the United States; and (c) sweeping changes in technologies from stand-alone computer and DVD video to Internet-based instruction and open courseware movements (software and even full courses at no cost on the Web). Given the perceived changes internally and externally and the requirement for self-examination for accreditation, an assessment was timely.

Highlights of the Chapter

1. A rationale was given for why starting a needs assessment and the nature of Phase I warrant full treatment in a separate book in this KIT.

2. Initial ideas were posed as to how a needs assessment starts, concerns in the organization, and the value of systematic planning.

3. From there the chapter went into an emphasis on doing one's homework and that assessments are negotiated endeavors.

4. Institutional buy-in and follow-through were stressed.

5. The discussion was tied to the three major decisions made in needs assessment.

❖ ORGANIZATION OF THIS BOOK

In Chapter 2 the first steps beyond the initial decision are described, including guidelines for forming a NAC and some strategies to get the committee oriented and engaged in first tasks. Going further into the phase is explained in Chapter 3. Collecting and analyzing additional sources of data are in Chapter 4. Chapter 5 is concerned with collaborative assessments, working in partnership with one or more other organizations. The last chapter contains the odds and ends of Phase I. Metaphorically, this book could be seen as taking the steps prior to launching the needs assessment boat, be it a mammoth cruise ship or a small dinghy. In any event, it needs to be a launch where you are prepared for the open sea, with enough provisions and know-how to make the voyage.

Bon voyage! Bonne chance!

2

What Precipitates Needs Assessment and Getting the Process Started?

❖ SOME FORM OF SYSTEMATIC PLANNING IS BEST

What event or events set an assessment in motion? There are no simple answers, but there are some general triggers that we have observed:

- a sense that the intended population is not being served or does not seem to resonate with current services;

- the problem is getting larger rather than passing or being resolved over time;

- the physical environment is changing, as might be the case with global warming, increasing traffic, greater demands for fossil fuels, and so forth;

- our market share is diminishing, and if the trend continues, we face major problems;

15

- a feeling is emerging that all is not right and the organization could be doing better or must do better to survive;

- a desire exists to improve and enhance our ways of operating; and

- combinations of the above reasons or other related ones.

Whatever the cause, the organization as a whole, or a group of individuals within it, comes to a decision (or a realization) that it will be necessary to explore issues and concerns. The exploration may be on the surface, but if the problem is large it will likely be in depth.

One theme noted previously was the human tendency to prematurely jump to solutions and in so doing to "short circuit" the process of identifying needs and methodically working through them to resolution. We seem to be wired that way, particularly certain individuals who are antsy and constantly wanting to get into quick, ready-made solutions, rather than actually listening to the details of a problem. (Listening for meaning, wow what a concept!) In terms of planning, the alternative to snap decision making is systematic planning.

This type of problem solving is a thoughtful, deliberate, and methodical way of approaching issues and needs—that is, it is undertaken step-by-step. Notice that "problem solving" is substituted for "planning" in that last sentence. That shift acknowledges that the two processes are similar in nature and frequently linked. If you do one, you will also do the other. The act of problem solving often brings in a planning dimension, particularly when carrying out activities to resolve priority concerns.

Recognizing that time spent working on the wrong problem is essentially wasted, systematic planning calls for careful identification of needs and examining them in a careful, orderly fashion. This is the style of living that all of us espouse in principle—that is, deliberate decision making based upon thoughtful consideration of data and focused information.

❖   REALITY REARS ITS HEAD

But reality comes at us faster than this kind of deliberate planning process can handle or tolerate. Reality is more complex than our plans can accommodate, sometimes and often frequently. The child decides to go exploring the store on her own, we panic, and we rush to find her and bring things back into control. Or the dog bites the neighbor's cat, and we suddenly have a lengthy trip to the vet and required, unanticipated expenses as well as an irate neighbor to placate. These events were not part of the plan; they are the unknown, unexpected things with which we have to deal. Bringing structure to a chaotic world sometimes requires large efforts, as things cascade from one unforeseen consequence to another. One of the coauthors uses a daily "to do" list with two columns; some priorities are listed at the top of one column, but the other column is left blank to allow for noting and hopefully crossing off the unforeseen tasks that routinely emerge and must be dealt with—an idea credited to parenting author Eyre (1974).

❖ A DECISION IS MADE TO DIG INTO NEEDS

Returning to needs assessment, trying to decide when to engage in such an activity is a difficult decision for an organization to make. Often what has to be done is mandated from an outside agency (an accrediting body in health or higher education, an accountability demand from the government) or a legal requirement, and there seems to be little choice. Still, we contend that it is better to be proactive than reactive and to begin the effort pursuing our own particular initiatives and what we see as important for the organization to do.

We move in this direction manifestly. Some groups may procrastinate, and that can result in a worsened situation, especially when the reason for performing a needs assessment becomes painfully obvious. Whatever the set of circumstances, moving forward is now advisable and should not be delayed any longer. What does this entail?

❖ LEADERSHIP: THE ROLE OF THE NEEDS ASSESSMENT FACILITATOR

The facilitator of the assessment (an external consultant or an internal staff member chosen or drafted into the assignment) plays a key role. This person takes charge of organizing and carrying out the investigation, with the authorization and support of the administration, other individuals and groups within the organization, and, in some cases, key stakeholders such as local businesses and civic committees. The endorsement and backing of the chief administrator and those who make critical decisions within an agency or institution are vital. There has to be buy-in at the start (and it is even better if there is a widespread basis of support across the organization for this kind of self-study).

What does this mean other than providing a formal charge to do the assessment or at least explore the possibility of doing it? Other essential features are

- having adequate time to carry out a defensible look at problems or understanding the limitations of what can be accomplished with a shorter time allocation;

- being supplied with sufficient resources to carry out the assignment and make a difference;

- being able to draw upon the time of the people you will interview or survey and being able to assume that they will view the area of concern as important and be willing to supply perceptions regarding it; and

- working with competent people to guide the activity (they must value it enough to fit it into their schedules and to commit their time and energy to seeing it through to completion).

All of these factors come into play and are positively affected by administrators openly supporting the assessment as a way to help the organization progress and improve. Without this kind of stance, there will be less than enthusiastic participation by staff, and given the nature of social environments, they might even write off personal investment in the process. In the extreme they could, in a subtle manner, sabotage the endeavor or kill it with indifference.

The facilitator has the challenge of getting the project underway and "keeping the ball rolling." In some situations, when opposition arises or comes from long-standing conflicts between individuals in different sectors of the organization or within one of its areas, having the energy to push on to complete the needs assessment requires almost superhuman strength and willpower. But that is part of the leadership role with the leader striving to build ownership and continued investment in the process and its results.

The leader may have to (a) convince (or, better, *reinforce*) administrators and influential staff about the rationale for looking into needs in the first place, (b) remind members of the needs assessment committee (NAC) that their efforts will make a difference, (c) help people supplying data realize that their input is important, and finally (d) make sure that stakeholders know that the process will be thorough and that identified needs will be important. This sort of advocacy is not for the faint of heart! (An illustration of this recently arose in a child welfare organization where administrators felt that some kind of assessment was called for, but they were not clear as to what should be done. From their answers to a few questions, it was obvious that they did not have full understanding of what needs are or what the process for examining them is. It fell to the facilitator, who was internal to the organization, to educate them and make a strong case for such a course of action.) As the facilitator of an assessment, you have to be sure of yourself and confident in order to convey the sense of value to others.

Part of a strong position is the knowledge and experience that comes with practice. The other books in this KIT contain many examples of getting the NAC and the organization working at this level. Use them and past work you have done as they fit into the context of this local situation. One of the first issues in the assessment process is to form an NAC. This seemingly simple step is one of the most crucial ones.

❖ THE NEEDS ASSESSMENT COMMITTEE

Purposes

The goals for the group (it might be a planning committee or have some other name) are multiple:

- guiding and reviewing progress at various points;
- certifying the quality and integrity of what is being done;
- helping conduct activities (playing an active role and even participating in data collection where possible); and
- serving as communicators/advocates to the organization, being a noticeable part of the public face of the assessment.

The people chosen for the committee should be competent in their areas of expertise and should have the credibility and persuasiveness to stand up for actions taken in the study. They often will present ideas to the organization. They make an abstract process real and adaptable to the contours of the organizational landscape. They may be in formal leadership roles or it may be better to use highly respected individuals who are the informal influences or opinion leaders in the organization. (See Altschuld & Lepicki, in press, for ideas regarding members of the committee.)

There may be times when an existing task force can be given the added responsibility of being the NAC. Caution, however, must be exercised in (a) not giving members of that committee additional tasks to which they are not committed and (b) not overloading already crowded schedules and responsibilities. Generally, the job of assessment will be sufficiently large to recommend the establishment of a new committee, rather than adding responsibilities to an existing one.

Membership

The appointment of an NAC is important for an effort that is balanced, meets solid professional standards of performance, and is acceptable to those who will use its outcomes. Exercise care in determining who will serve and in obtaining their acceptance for the assignment. Getting the right people cannot be overemphasized.

Considerations in Selecting Members

A key consideration is that NAC members are representative of the constituencies who will benefit from the needs assessment or that they are the individuals who will eventually deal with strategies (solutions) to resolve the needs uncovered and prioritized. The group should be a cross section of the organization.

In the same breath, representation cannot be thought about without dealing with the size of the group—what works best, large or small groups? What are the arguments for and against the two choices? A small group is less of a hassle to convene and manage. It is easier for the facilitator to instruct and work with a smaller number of people. Conversely, while a large group is more cumbersome, it has more capacity for carrying out surveys or locating data, especially when a good portion of the workload is expected to be borne by the NAC.

Furthermore, if this group prioritizes needs, there is value in having more people involved and more constituencies represented. It is recommended that factors such as these are thought about and that decisions be reflected in the size of the NAC. The nature of the needs to be looked at and the scope of the assessment are keys in determining size.

A small NAC might have 5–8 people, possibly up to 10; a larger one might have 12–25. Additional thoughts about this are provided later in this chapter. Regardless of size, members coming from the following types of areas are recommended:

- oversight boards, which provide liaison between policy and administration and are a means of contact across sectors within the community;

- community leaders who have additional links to the community;

- decision makers or, better yet, those who tie into or influence decision making (choose wisely since this linkage could be considered a constraint by some members of the committee and could inhibit discussion);

- classified staff to ensure that their voice is not only heard but also given respect in the role they will eventually play in implementing solutions;

- business department personnel who understand fiscal aspects of the needs identified;

- perhaps a few individuals with expertise in the area being studied but who are not narrow in opinion and cannot openly and honestly deal with new and different ideas; and

- Level 2 staff members (those directly delivering service to Level 1, receivers of same).

If the setting for the assessment is public education, the following additional sectors would be worth thinking about:

- teaching staff or those with close ties to the classroom;

- the curriculum department, in regard to its knowledge of all levels of the curriculum;

- the principal's office if not included before;

- students, particularly those who are mature and articulate (of course this would depend on the level of focus—high school vs. elementary school); and

- other individuals.

Analogously, in your situation think about what groups could be helpful in implementation or for the public face of the endeavor. They might be

- librarians (head librarian, members of different staffs including reference, circulation, cataloging, and classification specialists);

- hospital personnel (administrators, representatives from different staff areas, e.g., intensive care, hematology, neonatal care, etc., and from different professions, e.g., doctors, nurses, clerical staff, etc.);

- government (elected officials, division heads, or individuals functioning as head of particular areas, fiscal, planning, and research and evaluation);

- experienced personnel in agencies such as supervisors with good understanding of how things get done, problems encountered, the nature of the clientele being served, and what might be useful to the organization in terms of data;

- members of the population that is receiving services especially when the assessment is for a social service;

- key staff members in divisions of companies; and

- major customers or consumers of goods, suppliers involved with the company, and other critical stakeholders (more so for businesses).

There usually is a small group of individuals who could be identified from the organizational chart or would be well known in the organization and frequently mentioned as good candidates for the committee. But in forming the NAC, also think about representatives whose roles cut across departmental lines and/or external constituencies. There are some who function as generalists with an organization-wide perspective that might be invaluable for assessment activities. They afford to the NAC the subtle connections that exist in every organization that go beyond simply a specification of job role and function on that ubiquitous chart. Their involvement is suggested to build strength in the committee.

More Specifics About Group Size

A closer look at the arguments for keeping the group small or large goes something like this. Even though representation is a major consideration, there is much to be said to avoid the tendency to go large. How big the organization is, how its committees have functioned previously, and the nature of what's being investigated will be factors in establishing size. When a small group is appropriate, it usually results in less difficulty not only in scheduling and facilitating but in shorter meetings, since consensus will generally be easier to achieve. It does not take as much effort to get members appointed in the first place and to monitor the progress of work.

One advantage of the large group can be a bigger labor pool to draw from if the group will be helping collect data and/or find existing sources of information. In some assessments, the NAC will actually collect data such as senior citizens interviewing other seniors about potential needs in a medium-sized retirement community or students in a school helping distribute surveys and getting them returned.

Another advantage is that the group becomes the voice of the stakeholders in the needs assessment. Its members are the individuals that people look to as they consider whether they were represented or not, and the organization and its stakeholders will tend to feel that their voice and views were there in NAC discussions and deliberations. But there are always "buts." A very real concern related to the larger group has to do with how needs are prioritized.

The reader might wonder why prioritization is being mentioned for it occurs in Phase II or Phase III, not in Phase I, which is the focus of this text. Although it may seem to be getting ahead of the game, there is a solid rationale for bringing the topic up now. When choosing committee members, think beyond Phase I. You as the facilitator are in the best position early in the process to know what the scope of the assessment might be or become. If exploration of needs goes into Phase II and there are so many major needs that you are required to pick some over others for action, how should that occur, and who should make the choices?

A large committee representative of multiple constituencies would be good especially when prioritizing is to be done. Thus, charges of not fully including particular groups are avoided. This is underscored in placing needs in rank order and then shifting resources from one part of the organization to another. Without good representation, loud objections would be expected.

But from the get-go, consider what a larger committee might mean for the facilitator. It takes more effort and time to motivate the group and to make sure that its subcommittees connect and move apace. The demands on the facilitator should be included in the budget, as the job is more complicated with a larger NAC.

If the NAC will be prioritizing in Phase I, then a large group coming from main areas of the organization might be necessary, and you could use something like the Worldwide Model. Here is a quick glimpse at that procedure. Convene the NAC in a conference-like setting. (Preparation is required beforehand in compiling facts and values uncovered to that point and summarizing data that have been collected.) As an entire group, the NAC thrashes out at and "validates" one need. It is based on the values of the group, as shown in Figure 2.1.

The large group validates one concern, and then smaller groups deal with subparts of the bigger concern or issue. There are four basic tasks inherent in what is being done:

1. Making sure that the need is stated in a way that shows a true difference between the current and desired states;

2. Determining a level of criticality, from extremely critical to critical and down to important and unimportant;

3. Suggesting a timeline when the need could be addressed; and

4. Stating measurable criteria for assessing when the need has been met.

Figure 2.1 Concerns Analysis Sheet

Statement: Students in school today are much more likely to be overweight than in generations past.	
Facts	*Values*
1. Obesity rates in American children jumped 2% in the period from 1999 to 2003 (Chiasera, 2005). The rate for adults who are overweight is also increasing.	
2. Trying to lose weight is a national obsession. "More than half of Americans weigh more than they think they should," says Dr. Arthur Frank, medical director of the obesity management program at the George Washington University Medical Center. Each year, 15% to 35% of Americans go on diets, but no matter how much weight they lose, 95% to 99% gain it back within 5 years. "The body does a very good job of defending a certain weight" (Parade Magazine, Oct 11, 1998, p. 8).	
3. The number of students walking or bicycling to school on their own powers has diminished.	
4. School vending machines often carry high-fat items (and sell them well).	
5. Participation by children in unorganized sports (sandlot baseball, pickup basketball games) is less common.	
6. Parental concern for safety of children may limit the allowable activities.	
7. School lunch programs have less federal subsidy than in the past and face pressure to provide meals high in starches and fats.	
8. The increasing use of video games, computer activities, and cable television has led to a more sedentary lifestyle for most Americans. The phrase "nature deficit disorder" has recently been coined to characterize many American children and youth.	
Validated Need:	

Facts	Values
Level of Criticality:	
Target Date:	
Criteria for Resolution:	

Source: Adapted from *Next Steps 1.1–4: Planning and Quality Assurance for the Needs Assessment,* by J. N. Eastmond, 1973, Salt Lake City, UT: Worldwide Education and Research Institute.

By this means a set of validated needs is compiled, pointing primarily to only those needing attention. The group completing the worksheets could even be independent of the NAC, and thus their work would not be clouded by the previous investigation of needs (see Figure 2.2 for a semicomplete worksheet).

Figure 2.2   Completed Concerns Analysis Sheet

Statement: Students in school today are much more likely to be overweight than in generations past.	
Facts	Values
1. Obesity rates in American children jumped 2% in the period from 1999 to 2003 (Chiasera, 2005). The rate for adults who are overweight is also increasing.	1. While variation in weight and body size of students is expected, obesity is a public health problem in the United States and should be avoided.
2. Trying to lose weight is a national obsession. "More than half of Americans weigh more than they think they should," says Dr. Arthur Frank, medical director of the obesity management program at the George Washington University Medical Center. Each year, 15% to 35% of Americans go on diets, but no matter how much weight they lose, 95% to 99% gain it back within 5 years. "The body does a very good job of defending a certain weight" (Parade Magazine, Oct 11, 1998, p. 8).	2. Showing children how to live a balanced life, where exercise and nutrition help maintain a healthy body weight, is important.

(Continued)

Figure 2.2 (Continued)

Facts	Values
3. The number of students walking or bicycling to school on their own powers has diminished.	3. Parents should be encouraged to allow their children to walk or bicycle to school. School crossing guard personnel are important to maintain at busy intersections.
4. School vending machines often carry high-fat items (and sell them well).	4. School lunches and vending machines should help students maintain good nutrition. Foods judged as unhealthy, whether popular or not, should be eliminated from the offerings.
5. Participation by children in unorganized sports (sandlot baseball, pickup basketball games) is much less common.	5. Programs during school hours and after school hours should promote physical fitness.
6. Parental concern for safety of children may limit the allowable activities.	
7. School lunch programs have less federal subsidy than in the past and face pressure to provide meals high in starches and fats.	
8. The increasing use of video games, computer activities, and cable television has led to a more sedentary lifestyle for most Americans. The phrase "nature deficit disorder" has recently been coined to characterize many American children and youth.	
Validated Need:	Students at both elementary and secondary levels should develop healthy practices in both nutrition and exercise, leading to normal body weight for the vast majority.
Level of Criticality:	Extremely critical

Facts	Values
Target Date:	By January 2010
Criteria for Resolution:	90% of students will demonstrate fitness levels normal for their age group, and children measured as obese under current guidelines for body mass index will make up less than 5% of the school-aged population.

Select the appropriately sized NAC once what is feasible for the setting, what the group might be doing, and criteria for participants are established. Other criteria might be having worked successfully on committees before, knowing when and how to compromise, and willingness to hear and take into account the views of others. The final list of recommended persons is chosen, preferably by the facilitator and key players with names for alternatives, if possible.

Notifying Prospective Members

Contact potential individuals and solicit agreement to participate. Do this in person or by phone (or by mail and/or e-mail). They will naturally want to know (a) what the committee is about and its purposes, (b) how much time will be involved, and (c) what specifically they might be doing as members. Scheduling the first meeting should be mentioned at this time. If the person is unavailable, get an alternative member. A short example of an initial contact letter is provided in Figure 2.3. The letter could be longer, but the personal contact will be the mechanism for filling in the details for those nominated for the NAC.

Usually the nominees are "doers" and will be busy with other commitments, since many times they are already part of major organizational initiatives. In contacting them, explain why they were suggested for the NAC, what they bring to the effort, and why looking at needs is important for the organization. The contribution of each individual should be stressed. Nominees will know if the necessary meetings (probably one every few weeks over the next few months) can be accommodated along with current duties. It is important that a follow-up letter be sent confirming the time of the first meeting and describing in detail the functions of the NAC.

Figure 2.3   Sample Letter of Invitation

Dear [title and name of the person],

This letter is in recognition of your nomination for the needs assessment committee for [name of organization or topical domain for a given committee]. Your consideration of serving would be appreciated based on your knowledge, your experience, and the positive way you are seen by your peers.

The first meeting of this group will be held at [time and place], where you will be oriented to the task and timetable for this project. Please plan on about 90 minutes (1.5 hours) for the meeting. [If parking instructions would be helpful, include those here.]

The facilitator of the process, [insert name here], will contact you shortly in regard to what might be undertaken by the committee and to confirm your willingness to serve. We appreciate how busy your schedule is, but we do hope that you will be able to fit this important committee into your activities. If not, we certainly understand.

Sincerely,

[Signature, name, and title of the sponsoring official and the facilitator]

❖ THE INITIAL MEETING: ORIENTING THE NAC TO THE TOTAL TASK

This session is critical in that it provides an orientation to the upcoming tasks. It must cover (a) an overview of how needs relate to the entire planning process and why the organization now feels it should engage in needs assessment, (b) an explanation of the functions of the NAC and how it will be involved in the process, (c) how to deal with the preliminary reactions and feelings of committee members, and (d) the establishment of a time for the next meeting of the group. Here are some of the details.

Providing an Overview of the Needs Assessment Process

Members of the NAC should be briefed about the relationship of the proposed effort to organizational planning. A description of what might be included in an overview is in Book 1 of this KIT and in a briefer form in the introductory statements of this one. It will probably be useful to show diagrams of the full problem-solving process (see Table 1.1 in Chapter 1). If a detailed flow chart has been developed for the needs assessment in this particular setting, it can be helpful at this time.

In addition, the rationale of why the organization has come to a point where it requires an assessment should be explained. Why do decision makers feel compelled to look at needs? What events occurred or are occurring that precipitated a call for the administration to allocate funds for this activity? Is this a top-down activity or one that the administration initiated with the understanding that it is to become the purview of and owned by all levels in the organization? What might be expectations for the NAC, and what might be the outcome of the endeavor? What standards of quality might affect what the committee does?

The facilitator may have generally determined some of these issues via interactions prior to accepting his or her responsibilities. When discussing such things, it may be necessary to talk about bottom-up and top-down dimensions. If the assessment is very controlled and administratively driven, some of the NAC may not commit to the endeavor or may only participate in a half-hearted manner. In that case, soften the administrative role and stress how the work being embarked upon is the special domain of the committee. A reasonable balance needs to be achieved.

Up to this point there has been a lot of dispensing information and orientation for the NAC. The flow has been mainly one-way other than answering questions that members have. Now reverse that pattern to examine the preliminary reactions of committee members, especially if they are relatively unfamiliar with each other.

A useful approach in planning the session is to understand the position of those called upon to serve on the NAC. The undertaking is probably new to them, though some may have had experience with this type of exploration. Many are likely to be uncertain of their exact role, what contributions they will or could make, and what ultimate effect the results will have on the future of the organization. They have outside interests and may find it difficult to give full support, especially if the idea is foreign to them.

First answer questions with as much knowledge and confidence as you have concerning potential activities and how members' efforts can ensure the NAC's success. Specific planning has not been completed, and their help is gratefully required. Encourage them to express their feelings about the assignment at this time.

One other thing that might be necessary is to provide some orientation to the needs assessment process itself. This would depend on the sophistication and experience of the NAC. Several ways to do this are found in Book 1 and will not be repeated here, but one that is not introduced in Book 1 relates to the functions of the NAC.

Functions of the NAC

The NAC, as a sounding board for everything that will happen in looking at needs, reacts to the direction of the effort: how information might be perceived by the organization, the content and nature of draft instruments, methods of gathering opinion and/or other types of data, interpretation and distribution of results, and other aspects of providing guidance. The NAC makes policy and oversees all assessment procedures. It may also be an active body in collecting data.

Another function of the NAC is to serve as a check on the integrity and validity of the effort, something that is often overlooked. Any persons actually conducting data collection and analysis activities will come to the committee to describe what they have done or what they would like to do. In terms of validity, the committee reviews and asks questions such as the following:

- How would the organization respond to the methods being used and sampling?

- Will these entities be seen as credible and valued (do they fit the mind-set and expectations of individuals and groups receiving the information)?

- Will the data collected be useful for organizational deliberations and understanding of the needs of interest?

- How long will it take to collect the information?

- For what period of time will the data be useful?

- Do we perceive any difficulties in pulling the data together?

- How costly is this going to be, and if too much is going to be expended, are there ways to cut down on expenditures and still get what will be helpful?

- Can the data be analyzed in a reasonable period rather than requiring an excessive amount of time?

- Are there other things that we might suggest for this investigation?

- Are there areas where we should or might participate to help the endeavor?

- Are there other questions?

The tone of the interaction should be positive and focused on how to get the job completed. Needs assessment is both an art and a scientific endeavor. The idea is "how do we best learn about this area of need within budget and time constraints?" In its discussions the NAC must also attend to schedule and keeping on top of tasks.

Next Meeting(s)

Meeting 1 will probably be mostly for orienting the NAC to its responsibilities and specific duties. More detailed plans for the needs assessment, seeking more information, overviews and reactions to data collection methods, and related matters will of necessity be handled in subsequent meetings. The next one should be held within about 1–2 weeks. By realistically setting intervals between meetings, an estimate of the number of sessions needed would be possible, but be alert to snags and other issues that might occur. The general schedule shown in Table 2.1 will work unless the assessment tasks become quite large

Table 2.1   Generic Timeline for the Needs Assessment Committee

Session	Description of Typical Activities
First session	Provide basic orientation to needs assessment and the role of the NAC
	Encourage preliminary reactions of members and schedule next meeting(s)
Second session (1–2 weeks later)	Outline specifics of the local assessment (procedures and timeline suggested)
	Approve or revise draft plan for collecting Phase I existing data
Third session	Assign responsibilities for same
	Report back on activities accomplished to this point
	Show completed data collection and discuss preliminary findings and trends
	Continue obtaining data as needed and discuss whether more and/or different data are needed
	Keep collecting information
Fourth session and/or others	Continue activities of prior session as needed
Fifth session	Go toward one of the three crucial Phase I decisions: stop, initiate Phase II, or engage in prioritization and causal analysis as required for movement into Phase III, action planning
	Draft completed summaries of Phase I activities and prepare to meet with the organizational decision makers about them and potential next steps

or a fuller assessment is called for as the process goes forward. The entries in the table are estimates of the number of sessions needed over the course of Phase I. Some groups will use more and others less. Five meetings is an approximate number.

It is imperative that the NAC be a source of constructive input and that latitude be encouraged for those conducting the day-to-day activities of assessment. They must be fairly free to complete their work and not feel constrained or held back until the next meeting of the NAC. In practice, this often results in "leapfrogging" of activities, with the facilitator taking initiatives that may be approved or modified by the NAC after the fact. If there is continual waiting for the NAC to meet, important time will be wasted. If you are working as an external facilitator, it may be wise to have an internal cofacilitator who can be contacted in the event that an important decision needs to be made and who can give the "go ahead" or quickly call an impromptu meeting of committee members.

A follow-up letter to the first meeting is important. Samples are shown in Figures 2.4 and 2.5.

Figure 2.4   Sample Follow-Up Letter for NAC Members, After the First Meeting

---

Dear [title and name of the person],

This letter is sent to summarize the results of our initial meeting of the needs assessment committee. Thank you for your attendance and participation.

At the meeting we discussed at some length the reasons why this needs assessment study is so important to our organization. We talked about the likely steps that will be required to finish this work and specific ways that your effort can contribute. [Add in a few bulleted summary points from the overall discussion.]

Our next meeting will be held at [time and place]. Again, the meeting might last up to 2 hours. Refreshments [or lunch, if the meeting is to be held at an appropriate time between meals] will be served.

Looking forward to seeing you then.

Sincerely,

[Signature, name, and title of facilitator of the NAC]

Figure 2.5   Another Follow-Up Letter and Scheduling for the Next Meeting

---

Dear [title and name of the person],

Thank you for your participation in the initial meeting of the needs assessment committee on [date]. Those of us who were involved felt that the meeting was informative in laying out the expectations for members of the committee.

In the meeting we settled on a time for the next committee meeting [give date, time, and place of meeting]. If it is not possible for you to attend, please let us know.

As the person responsible for facilitating this meeting, I want to affirm my commitment to making this process a workable one that will provide major dividends to [the organization] in the future. This process should clarify the direction that we should take as an organization in the months and years ahead.

Your involvement is vital for the effort to succeed.

Sincerely,

[Signature, name, and title of the meeting facilitator]

❖ AN EXAMPLE OF WHAT MIGHT TAKE PLACE EARLY IN THE ASSESSMENT PROCESS

In the previous chapter there was a brief introduction to an investigation of needs in a university context. It dealt with a set of events in a department that led to an assessment as perhaps the best way to proceed. In some cases as mentioned before the real world is not an orderly or a neat place. See Example 2.1.

Example 2.1

Needs Assessment Being Demanded!

This was a department-level needs assessment. The impetus came from the requirements for accreditation. Further examination of the situation showed that an assessment would be timely based upon the recent, sudden turnover of the

(Continued)

(Continued)

faculty; changes occurring in the field; and high aspirations on the part of depart-ment members to maintain standing in unofficial but very real national rankings.

The change in the accessibility of documents via the Internet has affected the accreditation process and certainly what might be done in Phase I of the three-phase model. No longer does a mammoth-sized report go out by mail to an accreditation committee. Now, various key sources of data are placed on a Web site with reviewers examining them before the scheduled visit to campus. And even a special video presentation may similarly be distributed (CD or DVD), or there may be a streaming video on the Web providing a very personalized introduction to the report. When site visitors arrive, they are expected to have reviewed what has been supplied and to have their findings accessible (searchable), even in the form of notes, for the external report. The actual assessment described here was designed to be placed on the Web, as part of the "self-study" that preceded accreditation.

The NAC was purposely kept small: the facilitator (a senior faculty mem-ber), the department head, two other faculty members with strong research interests, and one graduate student representative of the student association. Scheduling the group required advance planning but nothing unusual. The level of "buy-in" from other faculty members was difficult to gauge although there were some seminar meetings with them. Part of the Phase I data col-lection called for a formal interview with each faculty member, usually last-ing from 30 to 45 minutes, conducted by students from research classes (expanding resources at low cost).

While the intention to conduct the study was announced in a faculty meeting, not one individual volunteered to get involved. Each person con-tinued to pursue his or her own agenda, with little notice of assessment activities, seeming to confirm an oft quoted statement by Clark Kerr, a for-mer president of the University of California system: "A university is a series of individual faculty entrepreneurs held together by a common grievance over parking" (Kenny, 2004).

As is typical in needs assessment, the facilitator and the NAC look for ways in which to extend resources. Fortunately, there were two classes of doctoral students who could participate in data collection—a small one (8 students) on the main campus and a larger class (18 students) at a more distant location, 45 minutes' commuting time away. Had the study not been undertaken in this particular term, the likelihood of class involvement would have been much smaller and the possible scope of the study scaled back. The facilitator's philosophy in teaching the course was (a) the best learning of methods comes from exposure to the process of conducting real-world endeavors and (b) an underutilized resource on any campus is student energy: Harness it and you can move mountains. Thus factors seemed to line up propitiously for this effort.

While this is a university-based example, it illustrates a lot about assessment thinking. Try to start afresh in the enterprise (a lot of information already was there via the Web and existing sources), don't assume you have to create much data at this point in the study, and find ways in which to magnify what are usually limited resources. This kind of action seems relatively easy to carry out in a university setting, so the reader might jump to the conclusion that it does not generalize very well. But in other settings we can apply analogous thinking as we scan the local context for individuals to help with the tasks that any such assessment will entail.

Highlights of the Chapter

1. The reasons why leaders and grassroots activists in organizations feel motivated to move ahead with an assessment were briefly described.

2. The emphasis on the concept of systematic planning is a key feature of needs assessment. Even though there is stress on the word *systematic*, be prepared for unintended snags in the process.

3. The role of the leader and the NAC are what make for the success of the whole endeavor, and as such they received extensive treatment in the text.

4. A constant balance must be made between administrative and high-level support for an assessment to include financial backing and then buy-in and ownership of the NAC. If balance is not achieved, the likelihood for change in the context is seriously reduced.

5. Procedures for leading the NAC and for conducting initial meetings were covered at length. They are especially important for starting the journey on the right note.

6. Last, a short illustrative case was provided for how one assessment began to do some of the ground work of collecting and thinking about Phase I.

3

Some Initial Phase I Needs Assessment Activities

We have examined the roles of facilitator and the needs assessment committee (NAC) in organizing and beginning to move forward. This chapter builds your skills in assessing the organizational culture. One perspective we advocate is that of an amateur ethnographer. It begins with a *cultural audit,* which is a fancy term for learning about the agency, institution, or business via an initial exploration as to its status for looking at needs. From there we proceed into other things that might be undertaken by the NAC and facilitator to firmly imbed the assessment in the context.

You are working as a facilitator (or consultant) helping a group of people do an assessment. An agreement has been struck and you have organizational support to conduct the study. It is highly important to have backing before going further. More than that, you have worked with key leaders to set up the NAC and are ready for the first meeting. You have done the appropriate homework about the organization and, while not as aware of all elements as an insider would be (unless you are internal), you have a sense of who should be involved and how the culture operates. Now it is time to formally meet and convene the NAC.

In the first meeting, welcome people and help them feel at home. It may be an existing group (e.g., a parent/community council for a public school or an existing board of management for another organization), and while the members are comfortable with each other, they will not necessarily be comfortable with you. (If they do not know each other, use an icebreaker to get on a more familiar basis. But let's assume that the members do know one another.) So this first meeting is an important encounter, and you and the NAC are aware of that fact.

Your task in the couple of hours that the NAC is assembled is to (a) orient members to the assessment and its aims, (b) enlist their involvement in carrying it out, and (c) give them an accurate picture of the amount of time and effort expected of them. If the committee members leave the meeting understanding the overall intention of the effort and their contributions to it, having made at least a verbal commitment to carrying it out, you have accomplished your task.

Going into the meeting prepared and knowing enough about the organizational climate and culture to function with ease and good rapport are very important. Here we ask you to view the organization with "an ethnographic eye," to understand values and to be sensitive to how they influence the setting. We note that negotiations regarding the study might be necessary for the facilitator as well as the organization to ensure that the endeavor doesn't promise more than it can deliver. It should be mentioned that Activity 1 might be done early in the process especially if you're a consultant and thinking about being the facilitator. It is a good exercise to see what the climate is for the assessment and to be on the lookout for potential snags in implementation.

❖ ACTIVITY 1: INVESTIGATING
   WITH AN ETHNOGRAPHIC EYE

Principles of Ethnography

Ethnography, which comes from cultural anthropology, deals with the study of a culture. It conveys the familiar notion of anthropologists traveling to an exotic land to study native peoples and report back on their findings about the culture, as Mead did years ago with Samoa or Malinowski did with the Trobriand Islanders. The idea that a needs assessor can use these techniques to understand an organization is perhaps novel, but it can be done and is useful for the consultant and the NAC. The latter would be particularly true if there were more than a few external members on the committee. Because we are speaking of ethnography on a small scale, the term *microethnography* is applicable.

The goal is not to make you an ethnographer but to offer guidelines as to this kind of initial probing. It leads to subtle understandings of the fabric of the agency, institution, or department and is very much along the lines of what evaluators do when they perform reconnaissance before engaging in an evaluation. They are trying to get a feel for what might be the best way to evaluate and how the organization might react to and use findings. Think of the activity as scouting the territory for needs assessment.

Working to understand a context has become a strong emphasis in evaluation circles (National Science Foundation, 2002; Thompson-Robinson, Hopson, & SenGupta, 2004). It has also caught the attention of business organizational consultants like Cameron and Quinn (2006). To do so, become a "participant observer" in the setting. The best observations often come from just "hanging out" or getting the lay of the land. Meet with various people, conduct informal interviews or chats, and record observations as you go. If possible, locate one or more "key respondents" (or "key informants") who can answer your questions or check your perceptions, to either confirm or refute them. You are doing this in a somewhat informal and casual manner, but it is deliberate, not haphazard. Of course, staff and others will know that, but if you go about the effort in a quiet and not too obtrusive manner, they will tell you a lot.

As you proceed, jot down a few brief notes on the spot, with the intent of amplifying them at another time (shortly after interviewing and observing). This will clarify impressions and force you to think about what is happening. Refer to these notes for future use. The frame of mind required to undertake this kind of informal study is one of "value neutrality," or "suspended judgment." As much as possible, cast aside biases and blinders!

People will be sharing confidential information with you, so respect what they have expressed and treat it in confidence. Certainly use it, but specific comments and ideas cannot be attributed or traced to individuals. Additionally, no unfavorable judgments are made about the context and refrain from making comparisons with other settings. Instead maintain impartiality while waiting to gather more information and have a more complete description of the organization—its internal workings, morale, the nature of the population that benefits from its services, and so forth (see Example 3.1).

Example 3.1

Viewing Through Another's Lens

One of the coauthors was part of a team conducting a World Bank evaluation in a developing country. He was not knowledgeable about the culture whereas the others on the team were seasoned international hands and were fluent in the language and with the country. He was not.

In conducting and later in interpreting interviews, the coauthor was frequently reminded not to view what was taking place through his cultural lens. This suspension of judgment was difficult for him, but as the interviewing process continued his interpretations as viewed by team members began to reflect a better sense of the culture that was new to him.

His first perceptions were that progress was very limited as judged against his Western, developed world criteria. He thought of the project as a failure. Once he could lift that veil he began to see that progress was being made, not in all instances but in about half of them. Compared to what were typical experiences even 20 years earlier in the country, this was a major change. Without the nudging to be more open-minded he would not have seen as clearly what was taking place.

It is interesting and worthwhile to note that as the coauthor adjusted his view, his interviewing approach became more adept in soliciting information from the interviewees. His framing of questions improved. In one case this led to some serious problems expressed to him in the strictest of confidence, which he honored.

In sum, we cannot totally divorce ourselves from our backgrounds and cultural lenses, but we can suspend judgment to a degree. It is wise to remember to consciously do so, and sometimes it may even be crucial to succeed.

It is important to state that "acculturation is everything," that you are trying to understand the setting of the organization as an "insider" would see it (Fetterman, 1997). Although it is not possible to fully view the organization that way, given the short period of time you have available, it is a worthwhile ideal. The more completely you "feel" the organization, the more effective you will be in relating to the concerns and needs being identified. The time spent in this exploration adds to the conduct of a successful assessment.

The Cultural Audit

A tangible product here is what is called a "cultural audit." This short (2 pages or so) document includes important facets of the organization's culture that you have uncovered. The four elements in it follow:

1. Organizational assumptions

2. Practices: formal and informal

3. Communication channels

4. Anomalies, problems, and exceptions

Examining these features could afford a better sense of an organization than even some of its members have. You are examining a cross section of the setting whereas staff may be more focused on their special areas than on the collective whole. Their views may be narrower with cross organizational perceptions not as strongly formed or held. Such findings may be illuminative for the organization.

Figure 3.1 provides a closer look at the four parts of what to consider in an audit. While it could require a sizable commitment of time, in most needs assessments resources are insufficient for this task. Yet even a relatively limited one provides insight into what is going on and what might impact a needs assessment. It enables you to see how it will or will not fit in or facilitate improvement and how to limit the scope of the endeavor to achieve utility and ultimately change. The entries in the figure are a sampling of probes for the ethnographic adventure.

Although an audit done by one individual in a brief period may not be comprehensive, it is still reasonable to expect something that is valuable. It can be enhanced through discussions with others. Figure 3.2 is a short cultural audit of a graduate program at a university, which subsequently factored into the needs assessment that was done. Figure 3.3 has the observations of international students in the program, and Figure 3.4 is an audit of a business enterprise. Figure 3.3 is a clear demonstration of how what we see is filtered through, intertwined with, and dependent upon a person's point of view and background (also see Example 3.2 on page 47).

An audit should be shared with the client, via "member checking," where the client looks for inaccuracies, misperceptions, or incorrect interpretations. Corrections are made, and discrepancies are negotiated. In the age of e-mail, if the client is prompt in responding, this is handled quickly, but it can sometimes bog down and may require considerable finesse. Face-to-face reviews may be beneficial depending on the nature of interactions in the setting. The audit itself probably gives a sense of which approach to use. The audit might be worded differently if it is only for the use of the facilitator or the NAC, with less

Figure 3.1   Aspects of a Cultural Audit

1. *Assumptions about the area in consideration*

   What are the motivational levels of people engaged in the area?

   How committed are all organizational levels to the assessment?

   What are the expectations of performance?

   What degree of respect exists across the work (concerned) units?

   How much understanding is there of what the others do?

   What are the opportunities for initiative within a collective framework?

2. *What are the common practices now done in the area?*

   How are services or products commonly delivered?

   How are audiences/clients contacted?

   What is the nature of these interactions?

   How are funds handled and distributed?

   Where are the shortfalls in terms of funds?

   What other related questions and ideas remain?

3. *Communication channels*

   Do staff members and administrators know and understand each other?

   To what extent does a spirit of cooperation exist?

   How hierarchical is the communication?

   Is communication reasonable without overclogging channels (the "wheat" generally comes through rather than the "chaff")?

   How open is the communication environment, and how comfortable are people with sharing private or personal information?

   How healthy is the climate for communication (positive rather than negative)?

   What other related questions, ideas, and perspectives exist?

4. *Anomalies, problems, and exceptions*

   Are there any unrealistic expectations by members of the organization?

   Are there cliques or groups that make people feel uncomfortable beyond those in a normal workplace environment?

   Does the organization provide enough time to adjust to new initiatives?

   Is it OK to challenge ideas without feeling intimidated?

   Are there any factors that work against attaining collective goals?

   What other related questions and ideas remain?

Figure 3.2 Summarized Cultural Audit of an Academic Department

---

Cultural Audit: Instructional Technology Department (October 2003)

1. Assumptions: faculty and students

- There is an implicit assumption that people are motivated to accomplish things on their own (faculty/students).
- The required educational level at graduate school means that you can assume people are fairly bright (can discuss issues, can write).
- Cooperation is valued, and excessive competition is viewed unfavorably (group work and quality of effort are valued).
- High performance is expected and usually delivered.
- Reputation among peers is important.
- Respect is important (people are diplomatic in referring to others).
- There is a low (or nonexistent) failure rate among students (MS/PhD).
- Faculty should be able to teach, publish, and do scholarly work.
- Evaluation is primarily based upon products—articles published, assignments—that is, portfolio assessment. (Tenure for faculty comes after 6 years. The evaluation for faculty afterward is less rigorous.)

2. Practices: formal and informal

- Portfolio assessment is pervasive; the quality of work that you can show an employer counts.
- Few written tests are given, especially final tests (results are demonstrated by project-based work instead).
- Lots of effort is made to connect with the real world (job hiring, consulting, class projects).
- It's OK to be paid for work even if connected with a class assignment.
- Grading is generally B or above with a lot of work required.
- Interaction between faculty, PhD-level students, and master's students is encouraged (though less available for off-campus students).
- The cohort system means you get to know a certain group of people fairly well as you progress with them through a degree program.
- Funding from outside contracts and grants has a lot to do with what happens, since these often pay for student assistantships. Getting in-state tuition or a tuition waiver is important and is usually contingent on having funding from an assistantship.
- Socialization into professional associations is part of the agenda for the graduate degree.
- Getting a job after graduation is up to the student. Some advice is given, as are recommendation letters, but not much more than that (maybe suggested courses for particular jobs would be welcome).

(Continued)

Figure 3.2 (Continued)

3. Communication channels

- Students generally know each other by name, at least within cohorts. Faculty know each other by name and from mutual activities over time.
- There is less separation between faculty and students than exists in some other departments in terms of being on a first-name basis and being comfortable about going to another person with questions.
- Communication is less hierarchical than in some disciplines.
- Some of the faculty act as employers for students, and classes often act as a screening mechanism.
- Several mechanisms help enhance communication: the Instructional Technology Student Association (ITSA), the ITSA grad listserv, and e-mail between individuals.
- Faculty and students are expected to communicate through e-mail.

4. Anomalies, problems, and exceptions

- Unrealistic expectations for students can arise: You can be grad assistant for Dr. X but choose to work with different-major professor Dr. Y (it is more realistic to consolidate these commitments when possible).
- Doing group projects with international students requires editing by native speakers.
- There are no set answers (even solid definitions) in this field. It's hard to say, "Here's the right answer!" Sometimes you get completely conflicting requirements and opinions on basic topics with different faculty.
- There is an expectation to socialize that sometimes excludes some students (older students, those less outgoing by nature).
- Staying current with technology and with the industry presents a major challenge for all (Internet and software upgrades, etc.).
- A disadvantage of the cohort system is that new folks may feel out of place (or old-timers may feel suddenly like strangers). A cohort gap exists.
- There is a feeling that some people do work the system to get through too quickly (the "one-summer-wonder" syndrome).
- Religious differences between faculty and students can be problematic. Being sensitive is important in order to keep adherents of other faiths from feeling discriminated against.
- Having a faculty member with a reputation makes it difficult to challenge his ideas.
- Having many international students at a time of concern about national security (post 9/11) may bring in divergent views (which may or may not be welcomed by others). Having these students provides a window on opinions about the United States from the outside.
- The marriage pattern in the state (younger marriages) means that a larger percentage of grad students are married than would be the case elsewhere in the country or in Europe or in Asia.
- The program changes frequently (classes, core requirements, expectations), which can cause problems.

- The tools classes are quite different from the other courses in level of difficulty, grading system, and assumptions about preparation (different expectations depending upon background could improve this).
- Having an undergraduate minor in the field means that people will differ in their level of technical skills in the master's program.
- With jobs in the field so dependent upon the health of the economy, it leaves a feeling of vulnerability (maybe more coaching about job hunting skills, including interviewing and negotiating for salary, would help all students).
- The master's program is internally focused (few interdisciplinary options are encouraged), and few students come in from other departments.

Figure 3.3   Cultural Audit Through the Screen of International Students

Cultural Observations of International Students (Regarding the Department Cultural Audit)

- Faculty and students are more diplomatic (less blunt) in expressing disagreement than in some other settings (like our home countries).
- Students are assumed to be economically independent when in graduate school. In many other cultures (China, Turkey, Korea), the expectation is for children to rely upon parents' financing their schooling but then afterward to contribute financially to their parents' living expenses and possibly retirements (and parents, in turn, will be proud of children's accomplishments).
- Dating patterns and interaction patterns are different in the United States, with an expectation that both males and females will pay or contribute to the dating relationship.
- In our department, there are fewer women students than men (not the pattern for most other departments in the college, where women far outnumber men).
- There is encouragement to publish the best papers (with an expectation that students can improve papers with feedback).
- Grading is high, reflecting high quality, but is top performance rewarded?
- There is not high pressure for domestic students (but there is more for international students).

attention paid to expressing the statements in a diplomatic fashion acceptable to the client. Tact is a significant part of the assessment context, and one must be sensitive to the subtle parameters involved in presenting findings to the organization.

Attending to unobtrusive measures is imbedded in "auditing." For an illustration of a skillful observer of the unobtrusive, read Sherlock Holmes, the master detective, as he exercises powers of observation and deduction. Holmes might glean significant information from the calluses on a

Figure 3.4   Cultural Audit in a Business Context

Cultural Audit of Furniture Sales Personnel (October 2007)

We recognize that there is no single entity that embodies all the features discussed below. We tried to identify elements that would be similar for most furniture salespeople in most store settings, based upon contacts with some 5 local furniture stores and telephone contacts with 8 large groups of furniture sales personnel.

Underlying assumptions

- There are differences between large and small businesses and between family-owned and corporate businesses.
- Selling is mostly on commission, unless it is a family business.
- Benefits packages vary, but usually this is an indication that it's a career option (in some stores, there is little or no benefits package for salespeople).
- Value and price selling are somewhat different.
- More experienced salespeople usually sell on value.
- Turnover may be higher in the larger stores (in both percentages and numbers of employees).

Practices (formal and informal)

- Scheduling personnel to cover all store hours is a major concern.
- Training each salesperson requires energy and time.
- Where students are used as sales force, the frequent assumption is that they are expendable.
- Small stores require multiple roles for personnel: sales, moving, buying.
- Larger stores use more specialization: sales only.
- Larger stores can rely more on their name, or sometimes brands, and less on sales approach.

Communication channels

- There are managers, and salespeople report to them.
- If questions arise, salespeople first ask their counterparts for help before asking a manager.
- Communicating with the customer is all-important: Rapport is required.
- Effective salespeople must come across as knowledgeable and believing in what they sell.

Anomalies, problems, exceptions

- For many of the people interviewed, turnover is not a major concern.
- Some of these people, training managers, may have conflict of interest (i.e., if the sales force were to stop turning over, they would be out of a job).

- For some companies, hiring practice and pay schedules may expect turnover (and pay less).
- Some companies, like —, have unique situations (i.e., no salespeople).
- Searching on the Internet has made selling furniture different than it was before. Having a Web presence is essential for most businesses.

Example 3.2

Cultural Audit in Action

The cultural audits in Figures 3.2 and 3.3 were carried out for the department described earlier in the text and not for the needs assessment that was conducted. The data so generated dovetailed into the assessment and were shared with members of the NAC as a reminder of institutional considerations to be aware of when probing into needs.

The mixing of what was essentially a needs assessment and a program evaluation was not clarified to the satisfaction of the consultant. A weighting toward evaluation was evident in the posing of the initial questions by the department head, a career evaluator prior to his move to department head some 4 years earlier. The Watkins and Guerra (2002) questionnaire (described later in this chapter) would have been a way to make the separation between the two, but it was not used. Instead, the effort straddled the processes in a way that was expedient but not necessarily helpful for each. Maybe next time . . .

worker's hands or the care given to cleaning the fingernails. Although we might not be as facile at finding and combining clues as Holmes, we can learn to observe and use information gained while conducting assessment activities. This process is best described in the classic book *Unobtrusive Measures* by Webb, Campbell, Schwartz, and Sechrest (1969).

In this vein, Witkin and Altschuld (1995) stressed the value of such observations in doing needs studies. Are some services offered by an organization not being used? Is there something that we have seen that provides a rationale for what is happening? Are different parts of the organization sensing similar or different problems? Are they not communicating well? Is there sharply different thinking about current processes that keeps popping up, and if so, why does it exist? Do we sense in casual interviews that people have not wanted to provide their views? Does this unwillingness imply that there are hidden problems, a lack of openness, or both? Do some administrators try to steer away from some issues and/or problems to the extent that something is amiss under the surface? Are there sacred cows that are off-limits?

(If you are external, that last observation may give pause as to whether or not to continue with the needs assessment. If too much is lurking under the surface, doubts about being able to accomplish improvement loom large, and it may be best to withdraw from the study. If you are internal, such recourse probably is not available. What the facilitator could then do is try to focus the effort toward needs where it is possible to initiate some changes. An internal facilitator, being closer to the organization and personalities within it, would have a stronger sense of what might be feasible.)

Some of what we observe or are told about could be considered "outcroppings" (Fetterman, 1997). These are objects or events that "stand out" as we move about in an environment. Examples could be a poster in a hallway, drug needles found on a school playground, or written messages, like slogans on a poster or cartoons posted on someone's workspace. What these elements may do, aside from contrasting with the background, is give insight into values and issues of the people involved. If a team is performing the cultural audit and its members individually and collectively note outcroppings, they lend credence to audit findings, particularly where corroboration is observed. A large number of cartoons with biting humor posted about the office might help an investigator confirm a suspicion that tension between workers and management exists. Team members should frequently debrief, even if informally, to see if there are common observations.

In observing, consider what is *not* present. When one of the coauthors was visiting a school in a state where high-stakes testing was in the news, he did not see children on the playground during recess. Based on curiosity, he asked questions and learned of the school's policy of "no recess" that had been in effect for years. The lack of a familiar part of the day led to an emphasis in the final report on that school's environment and its effects on findings. What is not present is more difficult to spot, but be aware of such possibilities and challenge your observations in this regard.

Another pertinent aspect of the cultural audit is patterns of behavior: One skilled researcher, in trying to establish how long it took before an outside observer was accepted as a normal part of the classroom, concluded that the process took at least 5 days. After that period children resumed their regular walking route to a pencil sharpener, rather than politely avoiding the visitor (or being curious and walking closer to the observer). The researcher was initially treated as an intrusion until being accepted as "part of the classroom." Kumar and Altschuld (1999) found that returning to a site several times over a period of months tended to reduce the novelty of a new person in a classroom or social environment.

The point of these examples is that you can sharpen your powers of observation, as you become more experienced. You will be more in touch with the setting and more effective and insightful in observing (these skills come with practice). As the assessment is starting, what are other activities that might be undertaken? How could we proceed?

❖   ACTIVITY 2: SURVEYING THE NAC

The NAC membership was carefully selected for representativeness. Whether the group is large or small, it can be an invaluable, easily tapped source of information. It is eager to dig into the nature of needs. Why not use it as a fount of information? One way might be to engage the NAC in a discussion about the area of focus at its first or second meeting. That approach would work, but it could be enhanced by tying it to another procedure in advance of the discourse.

A novel option would be to ask committee members to *write a letter* to the consultant (facilitator) addressing various dimensions of the problem under review. This is a way of getting the group excited about tackling issues. It is seldom done and may pique group interest.

- What do they sense is happening now?
- What might occur in the near-term future?
- Why is (are) the problem(s) there, and what underlies it (them)?
- How big are the problems and how many people are affected?
- What is the organization currently doing about such issues?
- What might be barriers (staff morale, administrative support, finances, inertia, etc.) to resolving or improving things?

NAC members would be given some structure but have latitude in offering their thoughts. Letter writing might best take place between the first and second meetings of the NAC. That would provide some time to qualitatively analyze the responses to see what they contain.

Another activity that might be used is to design a very simple and informal survey to tap into the perceptions of the NAC. Like above, the survey might be implemented between meetings, or it could be done during a session with the committee assembled. This survey is for a relatively small group up to 20 or so individuals and is different from the traditional ones seen in many assessments that go to large constituencies. It is a quick mechanism to get the NAC looking into the topic of interest. In that respect, the aspects of this survey are contrasted with those more frequently used in needs assessment (Table 3.1).

Table 3.1 Comparisons of Survey Usage for Organizing the NAC and for Conducting Needs Assessments

Criterion	For Organizing the NAC	Conduct of Needs Assessments
Purpose	Enable the NAC to establish a focal point for the assessment Initiate a discussion on the part of the NAC with regard to the area Encourage exchange of views among NAC members	Gain perspectives about the area of concern in terms of what is and what should be Determine what are the highest discrepancies and a sense of what might be the greatest needs
Size of Group	The group consists of NAC members and will almost always contain fewer than 25 and frequently 10–15 persons	Group size will be large and consist of multiple layers of concerned stakeholders Some versions of the technique might just be targeted toward key informants
Group Selection	The NAC, although representative in nature, is usually handpicked	If possible, randomly selected from the constituencies of concern or purposively selected if the target group for the survey is key informants
Method of Administration	Could be done via the mail but generally will be part of a group setting	May be done in a group setting but predominately occurs via standard survey procedures (regular mail, e-mail, or Web-based surveys)
Types of Questions	Scaled and/or open-ended with open-ended perhaps being the most useful and more prevalent form	Scaled surveys are the main vehicles for responding

Criterion	For Organizing the NAC	Conduct of Needs Assessments
Question Format	Use of checklists as opposed to double- or triple-scaled items will be noticeable as will open-ended items	Extensive use of double and triple formats with more limited inclusion of checklists and with a few (emphasis on *few*) open-ended items
Validity and Reliability	Validity and reliability are not critical or that important insofar as the purpose of the survey is to initiate group discussion and thought about potential need areas	Validity and reliability are prominent due to the fact that the results are incorporated into and play a much larger role in final decisions about needs
Issues and Comments	The needs assessor or persons facilitating the process should always be willing to use creativity with the technique to spark initiative and deep thought by the NAC	Surveys used with larger groups do not realistically take place early in the process but later after much contemplation and focusing has been done by the NAC

Observe that the survey for the NAC is more cursory and for the purpose of getting an in-depth exchange of its members' views. It's a "getting going" kind of procedure. Checklists and easily answered questions should be used, and issues of wording, reliability, and validity are not crucial. At the same time it is concrete enough to serve as a trigger for an examination of the problem or problems.

Moving now from an overview, how should this survey be developed, and what should be its content? What could be done that is not too time consuming but that will kick off that meaningful discussion that is necessary to get needs really probed? To that end, in Table 3.2 an overview of alternatives for the NAC survey is given. The table contains guidelines/ideas for constructing the survey.

If you administer the survey at a meeting and there is enough time, have participants go to the board (whiteboard, easel pad, etc.) and in shortened form quickly write their open-ended responses to several questions. Then the group clusters the responses as a precursor to a

Table 3.2   Four Basic Survey Formats for Kicking Off Initial NAC Discussions

Format	Typical Use	Comments
Open-ended questions	Usually done in a small group meeting where participants spend 10–20 minutes thinking about an area and jotting down comments and ideas	Can also be done via the mail so there is more time to contemplate the area with the facilitator pulling together NAC comments before its formal meeting The facilitator may have to prime the pump by supplying background information, even some statistical data
Mixed scaled, checklist, and open-ended format	Very simple and easy questionnaire to construct Approximately 3–4 pages long so that the group members can easily complete it in 15–20 minutes Use it to begin a discussion by comparing answers and getting a sense of group perceptions	Ask about such things as how many individuals are affected, what kinds of services are being provided, current problems, etc. May want to cover strengths, weaknesses, barriers to change, and factors that would help move change along
More scaled format	An extension of the previous row with the idea that open-ended questions are quite reduced in number in favor of more scaled or checklist ones	Tradeoff of simplicity in response for deeper answers may not be worth it The format may not lead to or engender as much thought and in turn discussion for the NAC
Many scaling options	Use of Watkins and Guerra's (2002) survey allows a committee to quickly determine whether an assessment or an evaluation is the desired course of action Advantages are that the survey requires 5 or so minutes to complete, it can be quickly scored, and the group receives easily understood immediate feedback	Survey could easily be expanded to include dimensions dealing with future needs or levels of need Very utilitarian device

Source: Adapted from Needs Assessment: An Overview, by J. W. Altschuld and D. D. Kumar, 2010, Thousand Oaks, CA: Sage. Used with permission.

lively discussion. If the surveys were done between meetings, the facilitator might prepare a short handout for the intent of fostering a dialogue. This procedure works well and is recommended.

Figure 3.5 is an example of a mixed-item NAC preliminary survey. It shows how items of different types can be put together in a format that is easily understood by members of the NAC. This activity directs attention to at least some preliminary concerns. Be creative and adapt the procedure for the particular area in consideration and organizational situation.

Figure 3.5 Structure of the NAC Survey

Format/Content for the Mixed-Item NAC Preliminary Survey

   Title: Putting Your Two Cents In

Possible Question Areas:

1. In your judgment, describe or identify what you perceive to be the main problems that are currently being faced in this local situation in regard to the area of focus.
2. What groups or individuals are most affected by these problems?
3. If you were to prioritize the problems, which would be the highest priorities, and why have you prioritized them this way?
4. What do you perceive to be the root causes of the problems, and how amenable would they be to resolution?
5. What, if any, programs or services are being provided for the problems?
6. What is your organization doing about the problems?
7. What are other organizations doing about them?
8. Who is involved in delivering services?

   Your organization

Staff	__Yes	__No
Administrators	__Yes	__No
Clients	__Yes	__No

   Other organizations

      Repeat subparts as above

9. Is there a plan for working on the problems in your organization and across organizations?

   Your organization

      __Yes   __No

   Across organizations

      __Yes   __No

(Continued)

Figure 3.5 (Continued)

---

10. Is specialized training required to work on the problems?

    __No

    __Yes (briefly describe _____)

11. Describe specialized materials or physical facilities needed for programs.

12. Are there other specialized programs that you know of that could be used to rectify the problems cited above or that would be worthwhile to explore? If so, please describe them.

13. In terms of attacking the problems, what obstacles do you feel might be encountered?

    Your organization

Staff attitudes	__Yes	__No
Administrator support	__Yes	__No
Staff availability	__Yes	__No
Staff interest	__Yes	__No
Attitudes of others	__Yes	__No
Resource availability	__Yes	__No
Shifting resources	__Yes	__No
Overall morale	__Yes	__No

   Other organizations

Lack of prior collaboration	__Yes	__No
See above categories		

14. What factors might serve to facilitate resolution of problems? See above list or simply leave the question open.

15. For a moment look over your responses and add any other comments or thoughts you have about what might be needed and/or ways to resolve problems.

❖ OTHER ACTIVITIES

When the NAC is not very knowledgeable about needs and needs assessment, use existing descriptions or create vignettes

Throughout the first three chapters a subtle idea has slipped in almost unnoticed. Despite having carefully selected the NAC, there is no guarantee that its members will know or understand what needs assessment and need really mean. One of the authors has been teaching workshops on the topics for many years and is always amazed that so little is known about them and so many concepts are misunderstood. If the facilitator realizes that the NAC has vague perceptions, then some instruction is in order. What are ways to go about the instruction without patronizing the group?

Existing descriptions take advantage of what already exists for instructional purposes. Aside from the content in this book, in Book 1 of the KIT there is extensive explanation about the three phases of needs assessment and the steps necessary in each phase. Numerous examples of needs in varied fields and types of needs have been provided. Use such resources as appropriate to orient the NAC. Teach about the topic without being pedantic. Perhaps excerpts from Book 1 could be sent out for NAC perusal prior to the first meeting or between the first and second ones. The committee could skim them as a warm-up to what it might be doing. Or it might be useful to send an example of an assessment in a similar area as done by another institution. Any of these activities would give the NAC a sense of concepts, what types of needs it might be dealing with, and what other groups have done to look at discrepancies. Be cautious, don't overwhelm the committee, and ease it into the process.

If you go to the literature it might be possible to find a *vignette (or scenario)* about current or future problems or simply develop one. Vignettes initiate an explosion of thinking on the part of the NAC and can be used to demonstrate the nature of needs and how they are investigated. Several brief illustrations in assorted areas are given below.

- Prepare a short write-up of several pages about projections in the growth of the population of senior citizens in the next 15 years along with some discussion questions. (Will there be enough providers of services? How will Medicare and pensions systems cope?)

- If the needs assessment deals with health, generate scenarios about the increasing numbers of children who are overweight or at risk for being overweight and the impact of this occurrence on health care in the short and long term. (What about the potential of larger health care costs due to the threat of later, related diseases? What about the effects on the national economy?)

- What would be the impact on the public health system if large-scale terrorist attacks were to take place or, even worse, a serious pandemic influenza was to become rampant in the country? How ready are public health providers to deal with such possibilities? How would we coordinate the necessary services into an efficient and effective service delivery collective? (This type of thinking could easily be applied to situations such as observed after 9/11 or the massive earthquakes in Pakistan and other countries. It is notable that work like this is currently underway in public health, homeland security, the military, etc.)

- In manufacturing, look at the costs per American car in comparison to foreign companies or in regard to the frequency of repairs needed. Some effects of this undoubtedly translate into sales and market share. Questions could be raised in regard to such issues.

- Look no further than the newspapers and the bridge collapse in Minnesota (summer of 2007). That tragedy sparked numerous articles about the status of our infrastructure (bridges, roads, sewage and water systems, electrical grid problems). It would not be much of a challenge to develop scenarios in such cases.

These starter vignettes (scenarios) stem from a little homework on the part of the facilitator. Go to the Web or find some current articles and note the problems in a field that seem to be recurring or mentioned as possibilities in the future. Then generate short (no more than 2 pages) write-ups with thought-provoking questions. Ask a few knowledgeable people for their feedback as to whether the drafts are useful and appropriate. Would they be a good catalyst for getting a group excited about the areas of concern? Modify them in accord with recommendations and employ them with the NAC.

When the NAC confuses needs and/or needs assessment with evaluation, use the Watkins and Guerra (2002) survey

Watkins and Guerra (2002) observed that confusion often exists about needs assessment and evaluation. A consultant is called in for assessment purposes and finds out that an evaluation is what the client wants. To deal with this occurrence the authors developed a survey of 16 scaled questions (see Figure 3.6). Odd-numbered items deal with needs, and even ones are oriented toward evaluation.

Administer the survey to see if the group is interested in one strategy more than the other. The NAC takes the survey, its scores on the odd- and even-numbered items are tallied, and whichever is greater serves as an indication of what would be best for the organization to pursue.

The survey has been modified from its original form in several ways. First, since it followed only one model of needs assessment, items have been reworded to include a broader perspective of the process. Second, the scale has been reduced from 6 to 5 points. Because of such changes the instrument should be viewed as a draft at this time.

Figure 3.6   An Adapted Form of the Watkins and Guerra (2002) Survey

The scale goes from 1 = disagree, to 3 = neither agree nor disagree, to 5 = agree.

The task is or has been to . . .

1. Make decisions regarding potential utility of a new intervention (course, process, product)   1 2 3 4 5

2. Determine effectiveness of an intervention already in use   1 2 3 4 5

3. Make long-term recommendations for linking intervention to the organization's strategic plan   1 2 3 4 5

4. Make recommendations about an intervention that is currently being used   1 2 3 4 5

5. Ensure that all that the organization does/produces delivers added value for internal/external clients   1 2 3 4 5

6. Determine ways to improve efficiency of an intervention   1 2 3 4 5

7. Link individuals/organizational parts to overall organizational results   1 2 3 4 5

8. Arise from concerns about suitability of a current intervention   1 2 3 4 5

9. Identify gaps between current and desired results before examining alternative solutions   1 2 3 4 5

10. Determine what interventions should be continued   1 2 3 4 5

11. Solicit input from employees/stakeholders about new courses, programs, and so forth to be implemented   1 2 3 4 5

12. Not determine return on investment of alternative interventions   1 2 3 4 5

13. Identify potential results/consequences of interventions being considered   1 2 3 4 5

14. Measure/determine impact of current intervention   1 2 3 4 5

15. Make recommendations seen as leading to improved organizational results for external clients   1 2 3 4 5

16. Make recommendations leading to improvement without input from external clients   1 2 3 4 5

It would necessitate refinement for widespread use. It is brought up here as a potential way for sorting through what the group might want or desire to be done. Even in its current state it has utility for working with a NAC early in its deliberations and could easily be altered for specific settings.

When the NAC is not very knowledgeable about needs and needs assessment, use fun activities

Needs assessment is work, but play can enter into it. In Book 1 (Altschuld & Kumar, 2010), "The Case of the Pokey Elevators" is explained. It is a devilishly simple and quick exercise that shows how groups almost immediately jump to solution strategies instead of considering what might be the underlying dimensions of a need or a problem. Committee members enjoy the activity, and it enables them to quickly understand why it is good to back away from premature closure on solutions. It takes about 7 minutes to do. We have used it many times; the reaction is always a bemused grin, and the effect on thinking is apparent.

Big Bob is another fun exercise. Often when we think of discrepancy, we don't think of multiple "what should be" states. This was pointed out by Scriven and Roth initially in 1978 and then as reprinted in 1990. We can have ideal endpoints—what is likely, what is feasible, what is expected, and so forth. This is the essence of Big Bob. There can be differences in the "what should be's" and values, and clashes of values can arise in regard to them.

In Figure 3.7 there is a very neat way to utilize this concept. Ask group members to think of something personal that troubles them (having a clean house, exercising more, reading more, etc.). Ask them to place the current status on one side of a divided sheet, and then have them postulate alternative "what should be" levels. Encourage them to have fun with Big Bob (as in Example 3.3), and it could be an excellent way to get into organizational needs.

In a workshop, one participant focused on the potty training of her young daughter. The ideal state in this case was obvious with current status easily inferred. Certainly all parents in the group resonated with the minimal level she described, and the sincere empathy of everyone in the group was visible in their expressions.

Big Bob helps a group see that there are multiple, value-laden levels for many of our social and educational needs as well as others (what are levels of wellness). If time permits, go into some of the questions provided in the figure. Some might argue it is a waste of time to consider the ideal since we never will reach it. A counter

Figure 3.7 Big Bob Exercise, Discussion Questions, and Witkin's Ideas in This Regard (derived from Scriven & Roth, 1990)

Big Bob weighs 200 pounds and realizes that he has a weight problem. He talks to a doctor, researches some health statistics, and thinks about what he wants to do about the situation. He might write down the following:

His ideal weight is 165.
He would like to reach 170.
He expects to reach 185.
The norm for his height is 180.
And a minimal loss to get him out of risk would leave him at 190.

Obviously there are multiple levels of what should be, and values play a role in educational, social, health, and other types of needs.

Almost all needs have a relative, value dimension.
Your "what should be" could be very different from mine.
You may not be aware of needs but usually are aware of wants.
The reasonable person standard separates wants from needs.
You cannot absolutely define need.

Along the lines of Big Bob, take out a sheet of paper:

Make two columns for describing the current and desired states.
Leave enough room on the right side of the page to indicate at least two and preferably three desired endpoints or outcomes.

Then think of a personal concern or need and describe the current situation for it.
It could even be an idea such as a clean house, jogging, exercise, the quality of your car, and so forth.
What might be some of your expectations for it?

For the same need describe three ideal states: a likely one, an expected one, and what might be minimally acceptable (*have some fun with this*).
Repeat the process for a program, project, or concern at your work site or for your job.

Big Bob Questions

1. How could you use this concept in needs assessment questionnaires? (See Witkin's attempt below.)

2. Does it make any sense to push decision-making groups in terms of ideal outcomes? Corollary—what sense does it make to think in terms of minimal outcomes?

3. Do higher-level outcomes automatically lead to considerations of cost and marginal cost?

(Continued)

Figure 3.7 (Continued)

---

4. What are the programmatic implications of higher-level outcomes?
5. Do you think that posing multiple outcomes would resonate well with decision makers? Are there any examples that you might know of that would be useful?
6. Could multiple outcome states be confusing and even lead to acrimony and arguments for decision makers?
7. What about bringing values to the surface in this way?

Witkin's Example of Multiple End States in Physical Fitness From the 1980s (B. R. Witkin, personal communication, 1993)

Excellent program

60% participate outside of school at end of 2nd year
60% participate at end of 4th year
50% participate after 5th year

Adequate program

40% participate outside of school at end of 2nd year
30% participate at end of 4th year
30% participate after 5th year

Idea is still applicable today

Childhood obesity
Type 1 diabetes rising incidence
Childhood overweight
Adult overweight

Other Thoughts

Source: Adapted from *Needs Assessment Workshop*, by J. W. Altschuld and T. Lepicki, 2007, a presentation for the California Department of Aging, Los Angeles.

Example 3.3

Those "What Should Be's"!

Applying this strategy in classes and workshops has proved to be a good teaching tool and an amusing diversion. The first time one of the authors used it in a class he realized that indeed a "Big Bob" was right in front of him. At the break, that "Big Bob" suggested that it would have been more important to have talked about "Hale" or "Hearty" Bob. The teacher could only fall back on the fact that Big Bob was the creation of others.

In another class, a very busy female graduate student described working, going to school part-time, and taking care of a family. A clean house was very far from her reality.

Her ideal status was immaculate—everything was in order and in its place. From there, the lesser "what should be's" rapidly degenerated. Her lowest "what should be" was having a corner of just one surface in her home that would be relatively clean and that would allow her to complete her school assignments. She volunteered to present her worksheet to the class, and needless to say, they understood the minimal end state and certainly appreciated the humor and pathos in it.

would be that we'll never attain high levels if we only go for low ones. Would we be on the moon if we quit at suborbital flights? Don't we in education seem to aim for minimal competencies? (Note the questions by Witkin in the figure that pushed responders to consider different possibilities for higher attainment in physical education.) On the other hand, there are other positions that would legitimately ask about the feasibility or likelihood of achieving overstated outcomes.

Additionally, limiting the outcomes to minimums may constrain eventual solution strategies. If we just focus on the organization and its internal resources, then we are putting blinders on the field of vision. In some instances two or more organizations could collaborate on what they do in order to achieve much greater results than either by itself. Higher end states require us to contemplate solutions at the margin— what might be added to what we can do now to make the solution even more potent and thus have a stronger impact? This is an indication that for some needs it might be better to seek cooperation and collaboration in the resolution of uncovered problems.

Big Bob could lead to questions about how we determine "what should be's." In some fields they may exist (state-determined scholastic outcomes, standards for the operation of hospitals or management and service delivery in nursing homes). In others it may be necessary to generate what is important and acceptable to the group. Each study of needs is unique, and the decision to use existing lists of goals or produce new ones depends on the specific circumstances.

Big Bob is more than just a fun way to teach about needs; it has practical implications. Return to the figure and the clever wording used by Witkin to get survey respondents to reflect on different end states from "adequate" to "excellent." This is a more sophisticated survey style that could be part of our deliberative process as we think about what should be and how results might influence policies and programs.

When the NAC is getting closer to Phase II,
use the planning and management worksheet

As the facilitator, you begin to feel that it would be good to move the NAC to Phase II. Members have a solid sense of the needs of the organization to be explored. This is an ideal time to introduce Table 3.3, generated for a group new to needs assessment. To utilize it one has to essentially prime the pump to produce a rich set of concerns and data sources for the group. What does this mean? Assume that the NAC has been discussing possible areas of need in an attempt to focus its activities. Members have finally settled on one or two foci and now want to consider next steps for data collection. This is where Table 3.3 enters the picture. Concerns are really questions or issues that are imbedded in the main area of interest.

- What do we actually know about the clientele we serve?

- What do our services look like, and what are their strengths and weaknesses?

- What attitudes and perceptions are held by service receivers?

- What do our competitors do differently or better than we do, and are there changes we should make?

The one thing that you don't want to occur is to have members of the committee say, "Oh, here are the data we have now, so the answer to our concerns is readily available." This is to be avoided. Note the four concerns for the goal in the table and how they require real probing into the situation and data (some of which may not exist) that offer possible answers. The intent of the table is to force the NAC into deeper thought. Challenge it to be creative and think outside the box.

Also note that very quickly a group could generate a variety of things that are known and not known and possible sources of data to be explored. The hard data (numbers, quantitative) and those that are qualitative (descriptions, anecdotes) appear relatively frequently on such tables and indicate the complexity of many needs and the fact that they have to be viewed from a variety of angles. Last, some sources may be cheaper to use and others more expensive, necessitating the expenditure of more time.

After your group's table is completed, there should be discussion as to how much of this can be done. Are there some things that might be better for us to do now in Phase I or early in Phase II? What about our skills to collect these data or to find sources where the best information

Table 3.3   Planning and Managing the Needs Assessment: Data Resources List Format for Preassessment

Goal: To revise our curriculum in educational research, evaluation, and measurement

Concern: What do we know about our students and why they come to our program? How does our curriculum match up with those of other institutions? What skills and knowledge are our students using in their work? What skills will be needed in the future?

What Is Known		*Data to Gather*	
Facts	*Sources*	*Facts*	*Sources*

Past Students
  Degree levels
  Gender
  Countries
  Current jobs
Courses
 	
  What we teach
  How concepts relate
	Records
	Faculty notes
	Syllabi
	Syllabi review
	Group discussion
	Job opportunities
	Requests for services
		Complete listing of jobs held
		How training relates to current work
		Publications
		What other curricula and courses look like
		What our competitors do better than we do
			E-mail survey
			Collect current résumés
			Literature review
			Phone interviews of other universities
			Collect other syllabi and benchmark

		Opinions	*Sources*
		What current students think of courses What past students perceive as important and/or missing Why they chose us What their expectations are What other consumers (other faculty) think of us	Focus group interviews Surveys Phone interviews

Note: Additional columns may be added to indicate who will be responsible for gathering the data and target dates. (From *Workshop for Korean Educators*, by J. W. Altschuld, 2003, School of Educational Policy and Leadership, The Ohio State University–Columbus.)

may be located? The group makes a decision on how to proceed. The table is amazingly simple but very utilitarian. To aid you further in its use, look at Figure 3.8 and Table 3.4. The figure is a set of instructions developed for workshops regarding filling in the blank table shell. Estimated time for the activity is given but depends on the particular needs being investigated. It is suggested that Table 3.3 be given as an example for the group to follow.

Figure 3.8   Exercise Directions for the Planning and Management Worksheets

---

Needs Assessment Exercise

Introduction

As an example of how to get an assessment effort started, consider the completed planning and management worksheet (Table 3.3). The idea there was to come up with concerns for a goal or an area and then to plan how to collect information about it. Where is information located? How easily and cheaply can it be accessed? What are the sources of facts or opinions? What kinds of facts and opinions would be useful to know?

Concerns are not "Hey, we know what data exist, so that is where we should go." They are not surface questions but instead what we value and think deeply about and would like to understand. They are more problematic in nature and require that we challenge our thoughts. They represent problems underlying the goal or area.

Notice the concerns on the completed sheets. They require in-depth thought about the area and force NAC members to expand their purview. They will have to seek information that may be quite different from what they originally thought for understanding the problem area. It makes the group really probe.

The Exercise Itself

Given the discussion above, complete Steps 1–3 (15 minutes) and Step 4 (10 minutes), leaving about 10 minutes for discussion (Step 5).

1. **As a small group**, define an area at issue or a goal. It might deal with what we know about the problem, what is understood about individuals experiencing it or those trying to deal with it, what we know about contextual factors that may affect it, and/or other examples of your own choice.
2. Place that goal in the appropriate space on the blank form and then **individually, not collectively**, define or suggest concerns for it along the lines explained above. **Collectively** discuss the concerns and consolidate them into three to four main ones.
3. Working **individually**, identify what is known about the goal and concerns, what facts and opinions you would like to know, and what potential sources of such information exist. **Be creative in doing this part of the exercise.**

4. **As a group,** discuss the similarities and differences in your ideas.

   What are some of the unique ways of collecting data and unique types of information?

   What about the costs and time involved in collecting data?

   Could some things be done in a relatively short time at very low costs?

   Are there individuals in organizations who could easily provide pertinent information?

   Synthesize what you have come up with collectively.

5. Large group discussion of the exercise.

   Could you use such a table in your situation?

   Have you ever done an exercise like this to organize your thinking?

   Any comments about the exercise.

Table 3.4   Planning and Managing the Needs Assessment: Data Resources List Format for Preassessment

Goal:			
Concern:			
What Is Known		*Data to Gather*	
Facts	*Sources*	*Facts*	*Sources*
		Opinions	*Sources*

Note: Additional columns may be added to indicate who will be responsible for gathering the data and target dates. (From *Workshop for Korean Educators,* by J. W. Altschuld, 2003, School of Educational Policy and Leadership, The Ohio State University–Columbus.)

❖ OTHER THINGS THAT HAVE TO BE ATTENDED TO AT THIS POINT IN PHASE I

Other considerations come up in the discussion of the NAC and/or in interactions with key organization staff and administrators. Attend to them in a direct manner, keeping in mind the resources available for the assessment and the practical requirement to limit its scope.

Limiting the Scope of the Needs Assessment

In an article titled "Bringing Focus to the Needs Assessment Study: The Pre-Assessment Phase" (Witkin & Eastmond, 1988), the authors observed that there is a built-in tendency to expand the work entailed in needs assessment. Strategies to "downsize" the effort can enhance the impact of the study. "Less is more" because the accomplishment of a task of limited scope is better than a broader incomplete effort that "dies on the vine" or one that exhausts our resources.

The consequences of the wrong scope can be disastrous. If the assessment ends up consuming extra time and resources or sapping energy to the extent that subsequent activity is truncated or neglected, the effort will have failed, even though technically it has the earmarks of a superior effort. What good is that if not much else results other than the study report? In the Japanese-inspired world of "Lean Thinking," this practice can be labeled *muda* or waste (Womack & Jones, 2003).

An assessment ought to accomplish the task with the right quantity of resources, not too many or too few. One that is too broad tends to omit detailed scrutiny of specific areas. Data collection may get too extensive and out of hand. "It is not uncommon to overextend with a massive needs assessment and to be so exhausted that the subsequent planning process falters and dies" (Eastmond et al., 1987, p. 1). Part of this tendency comes from an American value to stay busy and to show that you have done something significant. A narrowly focused study may seem healthier but be so limited as to miss important needs. Even though it might be done rapidly, in fact it will also be wasteful by expending resources for something that is less than useful (more *muda,* say Womack & Jones, 2003).

Prior to convening the NAC the facilitator may limit scope by clearly conceptualizing what is to be accomplished. *Conceptual clarity* will arise from conversations with a client to sharing the vision with others, showing exactly what is possible and desirable. Another way to limit scope is by contracting for just X amount of work in Y amount of time, given a specific set of resources. A common practice of funders is to ask for more than is originally proposed. This is natural because the further the topic is pursued, the more possibilities there are to explore. A written contract is a way of putting on the brakes and saying that some proposed action goes well beyond the earlier agreement. Some general features of a contract are provided in Figure 3.9.

Figure 3.9   Some Features for Designing a Contract

Some Features of a Contract

    Brief Descriptions of the Following Categories:

        The Problem Area or Issue
        Purposes/Objectives of the Needs Assessment
        Procedures to Be Used
        General Timeline
        Necessary Budget
        Organizational Responsibilities/Commitment
        Other Things to Be Noted

    Overall Length

        Between 2 and 3 Pages

Be open to renegotiation if modifications are needed, and by having a written contract, a basis for doing so has been established. Also to reduce scope, implement timesaving practices. Sometimes these can be foreseen, but often they become apparent as the study proceeds. One approach, especially in Phase I, is to find and analyze existing data that fit the target area. If such data have been collected and datedness is not a serious problem, then use them. In a recent assessment conducted by one of the authors for a state education department, most of the important information came from the state's existing database. These data were accessed through computer specialists at the state level, and there was some time lag involved, but the amount of data and the ease with which they could be manipulated was advantageous—infinitely better than gathering them from scratch.

Along with use of existing data, employing group processes can be a major timesaver. Instead of written questionnaires for separate groups, use focus group interviews with each constituency to discuss the issue under consideration. This requires planning and scheduling, but the synergy of a group working together can be very worthwhile. An additional benefit here is that the group provides its own check on accuracy. When one person expresses an opinion that is not widely shared, it may be thoroughly explored in the group setting. This kind of check is difficult to do with quantitative survey data. The last way to limit scope that we offer is the idea of seeking allies for the process, through collaboration.

Collaborative Needs Assessments

Locate other organizations or groups that deal with similar or the same problems and need information. They provide more resources for the tasks to be accomplished. Sometimes this kind of joint effort is not possible, but the opportunities for benefiting from the outcome can work as an incentive to get others involved. Ways to do this are described in Chapter 5.

Highlights of the Chapter

1. A mantra oft repeated in this chapter and the preceding one is that it is essential to know and understand the organization that wants the assessment. That understanding is the *sine qua non* condition of the assessment.

2. To that end the cultural audit is an invaluable tool in the arsenal of those conducting studies of needs. Guidance of how to do it complete with imbedded examples were provided.

3. From there the chapter moved into taking advantage of the knowledge of the members of the NAC. Particular emphasis was placed on the use of a survey for this purpose.

4. Then a number of situations (lack of knowledge of the NAC in regard to needs assessment, fun activities, etc.) were posed in conjunction with activities to deal with such occurrences.

5. Lastly, the content was focused on the tricky issue of the scope of the endeavor. Keeping the overall task within bounds of rationality and resource availability is important.

6. The intent of the chapter was to set the assessment process on the right course with key tools (checklists and tables) to do so.

4

Collecting and Analyzing Initial Sources of Data

❖ BEFORE GETTING MORE FULLY
INTO COLLECTING PHASE I DATA

The needs assessment committee (NAC) has done a lot of good work so far and now wants to see what would be the best way to proceed. With guidance from the facilitator the committee should do a "gut check" before going further into Phase I data collection. This is to determine where the committee is and what might be its next steps. The questions might go something like this:

- Did our cultural audit give a sense of what the organization is about and what might be the best way to go?

- What do we feel we know about the area(s) of needs, and how much do we understand at this time?

- Do we have a firm fix on the critical need or need areas or at least an idea of what our focus will be?

- Looking at the products produced by our work, do we see what other information might be desirable?

- Do we have a feel for the array of methods available to us in terms of information yield and cost?

- When we examine and consider potential methods with their associated time and money factors, what information sources would give the best return on investment within the time allotted for the NAC to do its job?

- In sum, what do we really want to do from this point on?

In other words, "What is our game plan?" If more information is needed, the NAC may conduct a number of informal (although more focused) interviews or a group procedure such as a focus group interview. The group might seek existing information that has already been compiled in previous assessments or evaluations done by the organization or external reports done by others.

Other options might be to do some preliminary database analyses, work with the local librarian to locate pertinent sources, or contact people in similar organizations facing problems like those confronting our organization. The group also could do a brief literature search on the topic. (An expanded set of strategies will be discussed later in this chapter.) Given these choices, an advantage of having a committee is that it affords more resources to carry out such tasks.

Even a not-so-large NAC is a working group, not just an advisory body. Guide it this way from the beginning; set a tone that emphasizes this mind-set. Once a decision about a task is reached, the NAC may be subdivided and the work apportioned accordingly. In this context, the facilitator supports the subgroups, coordinates assignments, nudges (pushes and prods), collates information as it is collected, helps ensure that quality data are obtained, and serves as a technical resource person with knowledge of methods and the nature of data.

When the NAC is large (20 or more members), think of the human resource power that now can be applied to the assessment, especially one carried out for a large organization and a major set of problems. That power comes with the price that the facilitator has to keep everything on schedule and definitely do more coaching.

The facilitator fills another role that has a big impact on Phase I. He or she will be in charge of producing summaries of data and the assessment process. In most cases, what the subgroups learn is given to the leader in advance of full NAC sessions. Collated data indicate progress and create boundaries for the playing field. Needs assessment is a constantly changing activity. As the summaries become more complete they illustrate the dynamic nature of what is happening. To capture that perspective it is strongly encouraged that they be dated (particularly critical for tables). This allows members of the NAC to see how things are moving forward and as time passes they should notice a continuous narrowing of the assessment to a smaller and more prioritized set of needs.

There is another important advantage to recording what is happening in summaries. It is easy to get so engrossed in procedures that the larger picture gets lost in the shuffle. The findings of the NAC have to be communicated to decision makers and the wider organizational community. The summaries are part of linkage to many groups (internal and external). These documents (tables, short descriptions of what has taken place, etc.) are major features of the public face of all assessment activities. But they do more than that.

❖ THE AUDIT TRAIL

Summaries of the assessment process are integral to maintaining an "audit trail." This is something that the NAC and its leadership should have foremost in its thinking. It is a record of the key moments in the study and the products of the effort that should be preserved. There are a number of other fairly important reasons for having such a record.

One is to provide evidence supportive of the recommendations made to administrators and the organization. If the committee is questioned about findings, the record will be invaluable. The second reason is that of organizational history and memory. Without the trail it is probable that over time the study will become a faded memory of a limited number of individuals.

When a committee is formed years later for a new assessment, it may only have meager information upon which to base thinking about the current assessment without prior procedures and findings to examine. How do they relate to what we are thinking about doing at the later date? In some instances, staff changes may be so extensive that there may be no one who was part of the original effort. Without the audit trail it is likely that "the wheel will be reinvented."

When a new committee convenes, its members need clear ideas of what was done before as *possible* input for the new assessment project. The new NAC reviews documentation from prior efforts but not as a straitjacket that prevents fresh and pristine thinking. Make sure that this caveat is in place when looking at what is available.

What does that record actually provide as the organization is again considering looking at needs? Key guiding questions are given below.

- What groups were involved previously, whose opinion was collected, and to whom were surveys distributed?
- Were any major constituencies omitted or not included to any degree and what rationale may have guided the choice of those involved?
- What forms were used?
- What variables were measured or studied?
- How well might they fit the current endeavor or could they be adapted so we can save time and energy by capitalizing on what our predecessors did?
- Was any aspect of what we are looking at now dealt with in any fashion 5 years ago?
- Were there any specific areas not examined that might have pertinence in the changed environment in which we currently exist?
- What was found, and to what extent did those results lead to organizational action?
- If no action was taken, why was that the case?
- How successful was the prior process and what was and is the organizational perspective of the overall activity?
- What problems were observed in the past, and how might they be prevented from reoccurring?
- What should be in the current audit trail?

Take stock of what has been done and/or what is transpiring. A cultural audit has been completed; scenarios may have been prepared, and the NAC may have reacted to them; its members may have completed short surveys and/or provided perspectives in response to a variety of things done during the first few meetings of the committee and in the periods between them.

There are a number of products finished or that will become available soon that are relevant for summary purposes. The NAC is starting to amass much in the way of data, short reports, and so forth. Such materials and the meaty information they provide can easily get away from the committee unless they are captured in utilitarian formats. What might be there that should be summarized? It could emerge from the following.

- The NAC may have had discussions and located sources that are relevant to the focus of the assessment.

- Interviews may have been conducted and even some benchmarking activities undertaken by the NAC.

- A few members may have looked at hard data or done some database manipulations.

- Some may have worked with the local librarian to find interesting literature sources that will aid the committee in its deliberations. (See Example 4.1 for an illustration of this point.)

Example 4.1

Don't Underestimate the Power of the Literature—Even a Cursory Review of It!

The reader may have observed ideas coming from the area of aging earlier in this book. One of the authors was asked to teach a needs assessment workshop for the department of aging in a large state. While both authors will admit to having some years and meeting the qualifications for the aging category, other than that the field is not a particular emphasis for either one.

The coauthor thought that he was up to the task in terms of general principles but not in regard to detailed, specific special applications in aging. With the aid of a colleague (substitute local librarian in another situation), he quickly found 10–15 sources on the subject. Further, he observed that newspapers and magazines often carried articles on the topic as does the monthly he receives from a national association of retired persons (a transparently veiled reference that should be apparent to nearly all readers of this text).

From a quick scanning of such sources, he was able to see many trends related to needs. Just to mention a few, the population of aging citizens is expected to skyrocket whereas the corresponding numbers of well-trained care providers at a variety of levels will not increase without major interventions. Another trend is that there are obvious problems in the provision of health-related care for many segments of an older population. Lastly, most of our houses are built with families in mind as opposed to the needs of seniors. It would necessitate a retrofitting of virtually millions of homes in the United States if the desired end state is to help people remain in surroundings familiar to them as long as possible. (If there ever was a needs assessment topic ripe for picking it is this one. What do we know about the insides of current housing and how receptive seniors would be to investing in redoing their homes in this manner? It would take a great deal of information in regard to the "what is" state before meaningful policies could be developed.)

Mindful of the dangers of being xenophobic, it is interesting to add that the literature search found similar patterns in other countries. This is not surprising since many other locations are experiencing growing populations of senior citizens.

(Continued)

(Continued)

The coauthor used what he learned to adapt general principles of assessment to the circumstances of aging. Analogous to what would occur in actually doing a study of needs, draft materials were sent to the workshop coordinator in the state department for review (in needs assessment, the NAC would be looking at what is being created), and his approval and that of several others were obtained. In fact, they felt that the examples and case studies for the workshop were on target.

The bottom line is that the cursory literature review was an effective way to quickly learn about needs. When you can, see if some small amount of the budget can be allotted for this purpose. Doing so will almost always pay dividends. Lastly, observe that the popular literature played a role in what he produced for the workshop. (We will describe this type of source in greater detail under the "other sources" section.)

Returning to the audit idea, assume that a ton of information is there and the facilitator wants to create tables that capture the rich Phase I data findings. What is a good format for such data? What will be useful for decision making and the audit trail? Many options are possible, and Tables 4.1 and 4.2 are provided to show what such tables could look like.

❖ FORMATS FOR PHASE I FINDINGS

Tables such as these would be completed over a period of weeks (maybe up to 6 or so) and would represent compressed statements of what the NAC has been achieving and what has been perceived about needs. There could be massive amounts of data generated that have to be distilled into a finer potable brew instead of remaining in their original form. Summaries in tabular form aid decision makers in seeing the larger picture as well as some of the rich details of what the committee has been doing. As data come in, there would be updated versions of the tables, each more advanced (more cells being filled in with information) than the prior one, and each would carry the actual date it was produced. Documentation of the assessment process would automatically result from dating all products, especially tables.

A slightly different way of thinking about and then portraying initial data is to remember that in many cases the NAC at this preliminary

Table 4.1 One Useful Format for Displaying the Initial Work of the NAC

Area of Concern	What Should Be	What Is	Sources of Information	What We'd Like to Know	Sources of Information
Area 1 Subarea Subarea	Standards, expectations	Current status	Records, archives	More about status, perceptions of status, etc.	Other records, interviews, etc.
Area 2 Subarea Subarea Subarea					
Area n					

Source: From *Needs Assessment: An Overview*, by J. W. Altschuld and D. D. Kumar, 2010, Thousand Oaks, CA: Sage. Used with permission.

Table 4.2 A Phase I Decision-Oriented Framework

Need Area and Subareas	Further Actions Required	Reasons for Further Action	Preliminary Ideas About Causes	Solutions
Area 1 Subarea 1 Subarea 2				
Area 2				
Area 3				
Area n				

Source: From *Needs Assessment: An Overview*, by J. W. Altschuld and D. D. Kumar, 2010, Thousand Oaks, CA: Sage. Used with permission.

time may be just identifying concerns with facts and values. These may later become validated needs (those that have been studied in depth, verifying their accuracy, meaning, and importance).

So the data could be shown on "concerns sheets," which are displayed with "facts" listed on one side and "values" listed on the other, with a descriptive heading as shown in Figures 2.1 and 2.2. Gathering these sheets, filled out as much as possible, facilitates the work of the NAC. There are many ways to structure tables and figures like these, do not feel compelled to use ours but observe that they are quite parallel in form and draw off the concepts in the planning and managing tables described in Chapter 3. The ideas of values, perceptions, and hard data are consistent in the approaches.

Another general principle that is being followed is that there will be too much data and the NAC, the decision makers, and members of the organization can be inundated with all of the fine print as to lose understanding of the overall frame. We suggest that the broader view is more important than the fine details.

Along these lines, keep your tables short and to the point. The richness of the data is valuable and filters into the tables as much as feasible, but judgment has to be exercised as to how much should be abstracted from what has been produced. It might even be worthwhile to have the NAC role-play positions that might be taken by decision makers when they are reviewing the work of the committee.

❖ GETTING INTO THE ARRAY OF PHASE I METHODS

Let's return to a possible array of Phase I methods. If you are familiar with many of the procedures used in Phases I and II of needs assessment, it is to be expected that there is some similarity amongst them. While a few are unique to a specific phase of the process, overlap is reasonable. At times it is a matter of degree.

For example, database analyses in Phase I may be more on the surface of the problem and not as in-depth as in Phase II. You simply do not have enough time early in the exploratory work to really dig into the data, but often you can get meaningful ideas in a fast manner. What is this need about? Would it be worth the time and money of the organization to investigate it further? Does it seem to be important enough to go beyond Phase I? Does other evidence that we have collected corroborate a decision to push ahead with the study, or have we gleaned sufficient information to make recommendations about critical needs? What should we do next?

This process will lead you to three main choices:

1. Determining that this need should not be looked at anymore and explaining why;

2. Digging much more deeply into the need and describing what might be done with our resources; and

3. Proceeding rapidly and directly into Phase III—postassessment (action planning)—as Phase I has revealed that this is an important area for the organization to consider.

Frequently, the third course of action necessitates doing some additional Phase II study, but the facilitator, based on experience, will be sensitive to the situation and assist the NAC in arriving at its best and most logical conclusion.

Phase I is called preassessment for a reason. If the NAC does not feel compelled to look at any or all needs beyond the initial review that is a reasonable outcome. There is no compunction to expend precious time and effort when it will come to naught. On the other hand, the investigation started because of a growing concern in the organization about a problem or set of problems. Something is wrong, and we don't feel comfortable with the way things are or how they might evolve. What this implies is that more often than not the overall endeavor will go through all three phases of needs assessment—not every step and every detail but some aspects of the phases will be implemented.

What are some of the sources that help us and provide guidance for Phase I? They are largely readily available and would not require excessive time and/or funds to obtain. Don't create new sources and feel required to use them to obtain needs-related data. That is mainly the task for Phase II but not now. Also remember that if the data that we locate are unreliable or spurious, final conclusions based on them cannot be any better. This will always be a problem in Phase I.

Usually multiple sets of data are obtained and reviewed, and if they are corroborative, there is additional confidence that buttresses conclusions being made. What is being done is piecing together from surface types of data a circumstantial case for or against needs. If some data are particularly weak (not much reliability or validity, limited face validity for the decision-making audience, suspect due to size of samples or groups from which the data emanated), they may have to be omitted or dealt with selectively.

Sources are listed below with the acknowledgment that there may be other ones in your local context.

- Institutional data

- Newspaper articles and archives

- Past evaluations, assessments, or accreditation reports

- Unobtrusive data, skillfully collected

- Data from existing surveys, interviews, or focus groups

Each of these help in the Phase I effort and for the most part are right there or easily obtained. Limited costs are involved.

Institutional Data

For the past 2 years, one of the authors has been heavily involved in assessing the supply of and demand for teachers in his state. He found that, given the current rate of graduation of new teachers and the projected number of retirees, a shortage can be expected for at least 10 years and that, unless current policies are changed, it will compound, getting more severe each year.

Human resource studies like this are needs assessments. Reflecting on the study, it is amazing how much of the important information came from an existing source, a "data warehouse" maintained by the state. While a survey was used for part of the data, over 80% of the contents of the final report took existing data and presented it in a more readable way and with a new interpretation to it. One of the recommendations for the future was that new procedures for compiling such data be instituted on an annual basis, and suggestions were provided for exactly how that could be done.

The point is simply that existing data represent a wealth of information that ought not to be overlooked as an assessment gets underway. This example easily generalizes to a variety of fields. Where do the data reside? To what extent are they accessible? Are there individuals who can quickly assist in producing initial information for the NAC? What basic questions should be asked of the base, and can it provide appropriate answers to them?

In education, most local systems have tons of information that often will be provided by their research, evaluation, and/or planning offices upon request. (Use appropriate safeguards for protecting the rights of individuals when accessing sources.) Every U.S. state collects and maintains standardized testing results that can be aligned with demographic characteristics of school districts (see Example 4.2).

Example 4.2

Using a Higher Education Database in a Basic Quick Phase I Exploration

Higher education has extensive amounts of data and documentation readily available. In fact, so much is there that one has to step back for a moment and think what would be the best (and in Phase I probably simple and direct) questions to ask. This was exactly what was done by a statewide consortium of universities involved in minority student retention in STEM (science, technology, engineering, and mathematics) disciplines.

More specifically in one aspect of their work, consortium members were concerned with how many doctorates were earned by minority students in the appropriate fields. They knew that the state collected such data and made it accessible. So a request was made to the state's higher education authorities.

"Can you tell us how many minority PhDs are graduating each year across the member institutions of the consortium, and can you do that for every year since 2000 or thereabouts?"

The answer was yes, and it was a relatively direct matter to do so. These data were incorporated into a straightforward table generated for a proposal submission regarding the recruitment of minority students for a STEM doctoral study. The shell shown below displays the general nature of the table and how valuable the simplified portrayal of the situation could be. Since the proposal was relatively short, one or two tables like this within it were sufficient to demonstrate a possible need, at least on a surface level. The trick was to ask a basic question that showed what was happening or not happening in the member institutions. (By the way, rather small numbers of graduates were observed.)

A Possible Table Shell for Doctoral Graduation Data

Institution	Year 1	Year 2	Year n	Total
Institution 1				
Institution 2				
Institution 3				
Institution n				
	Total Year 1	Total Year 2	Total Year n	Grand Total

The table was perfect for presenting data describing the "what is" status of minority doctorates, the pattern of graduation rates over the years, and

(Continued)

(Continued)

what was happening at individual universities. In terms of a more expanded assessment of needs, notice that many other more probing questions could have been raised and indeed are probably necessary for Phase II.

- Which specific minorities are attaining the doctorate, and in what fields?
- What is the makeup of graduates in terms of gender?
- How many of these former students are native to the state, and how many come from elsewhere?
- Where are they now, and how many are working in industry in their areas of specialty?
- How many are university faculty?
- What other types of work are they doing?
- How many have stayed in the state, and what were their reasons for doing so?
- Is there any long-term follow-up going on in regard to these former students, and if so, what do we know about them?

Going to more probing questions occurs as we go further in examining needs, usually in Phase II, and may lead us to the conclusion that not all information required to understand needs will come from the database. It is often the case that data from quantitative sources (databases, test results, number counts, surveys) and from qualitative ones (observations, groups processes, and the like) are necessary to understand needs with the corollary that such understanding only emerges from multiple sources and different perspectives. In this respect, some needs are complex.

Most of the preceding discussion about databases comes from educational cases. Think about generalizing to other areas. Database information can be located in state and local public health records that are routinely maintained. Census and other records can be found in regard to mental health, aging, sales figures, the nature of the workforce, migration rates, obesity, disease rates, and so forth.

Newspapers and Related Sources

Other sources are newspapers and similar public types of entities (refer to Example 4.1 where some magazine and newsletter articles were used for the aging workshop). Sometimes institutions (school systems, public agencies, company public relations offices, etc.) routinely monitor what is being said about them. If you know the setting, it may be possible to get at such information very quickly. It is a kind of unob-trusive measure of the "what is" status as perceived by external eyes. One would use these data in conjunction with additional sources. But since they are readily available, their use is recommended.

Ask project staff members if they have been keeping a "clip file." Almost all programs do. It is a compilation of media representations of the endeavor. Often, newspaper articles or television coverage of the program will be fairly easy to pull off the shelves, especially if you have established a sufficiently high level of trust with staff members. (Trust is necessary because there may be some negative views of the program and there is a natural reluctance to share these.) Besides tra-ditional media, factor in any project-developed Web sites or other ori-enting information.

What can be learned from news-related items? A newspaper article may be or have within it an encapsulated snapshot of some aspect of the project or program, depicted from the viewpoint of an observer or a reporter. If the story was generated from within the organization, it will likely provide an account of the organization's accomplishments (possibly overstated but still information about the need area).

When self-generated by the project, the perceptions reported will likely be shared by at least some of the leaders in the organization. If the items appeared over a period of time, they provide some notion of the growth/progress of the organization.

In this age of electronic media, access to newspaper files as well as other information is more online, and searching for specific project information is easier. Computer search strategies allow for access to past information. These news and media sources give one perspective on the program that can help in any assessment.

Also consider magazine articles about the general need being stud-ied. Current problems are constantly being talked about in the popular press. Journals or magazines put out by national public interest groups that are intended for lay consumption can be invaluable for needs assessment. These may help the organization obtain a broader sense of the discrepancy or gap and how the local situation might be a reflection of a national concern. It gives a backdrop to the problem. What are oth-ers saying about it, and what are their views? How are other locations coping with it and to what degree do they seem similar to our setting?

Past Work Done in the Organization

We should not rely solely on sources such as those just given above. Most organizations may have done a needs assessment or a related study in the past. Again the audit trail is a valuable source, and it's free of charge. Better yet, are some of the individuals who worked on assessing needs before available for discussion? Chat with them, most likely on an informal basis. Engage them in a friendly way.

- What are their recollections?

- What did the process produce?

- What problems, if any, did they encounter, and what might be avoided this time?

- Were there needs that they thought were missed or that have become more important over time?

- How did the organization respond to what was done?

- What do they think about the current organizational climate (personnel, nature of decision making, etc.) for this new assessment?

- What were the results of the prior work?

- If it was not successful, why, and what should be avoided?

Be open about the chats—let individuals expound about their recollections. This exchange should prove informative about what to do in the current circumstance.

Beyond this, were there any evaluations done in this area, and are the reports available? If so, is the organization or individuals willing to share them? Review them with the view that you are in a dynamic situation. What can be gleaned from the past that will be applicable to the present or near-term future? Be especially alert to findings, recommendations, methods, variables, and measuring strategies.

Since the assessment of needs is less common than program and project evaluation, it is more likely that the latter will be there. The two entities are related processes. The assessment will be much more on the front (planning) end of a new program or project whereas the evaluation will be to see if the solution is working as planned and to determine whether outcomes were achieved by it. The needs uncovered and the outcomes being assessed have related elements and features.

Look at the evaluation in regard to what the dependent or outcome variables were. How were they measured? To what extent were the needs for which the project was funded and implemented met? What groups were impacted by it? What groups were not? If funding was discontinued, why was that the case, and what led to this decision?

What is the relevance of this information for what we might do in the present instance?

In education there are special studies that may have been commissioned and accreditations of school systems with formal documentation of findings. Ask if they are accessible. In public health, medical care, social services, and business, periodic checks are carried out in regard to standards and/or progress toward goals being made. As an example, hospitals and health care types of organizations routinely undergo accreditation procedures. What were the findings, to what extent were troublesome situations rectified (or do they still remain areas of need), are there parts of the reports that are pertinent to the proposed area of the assessment, and so forth? Look for places where evaluative findings may have been ignored. Doing so (i.e., ignoring information) may be OK in the short run but over the long haul may in some circumstances imperil the existence of the organization. It is important to examine all such sources of information, even if superficially, for they may be relevant.

Unobtrusive Measures

In Phase I you will be informally chatting with a number of different individuals from varying levels in and outside of the organization. One aspect of doing this would be to carefully observe how people are responding to the interviews. Do they seem uptight and terse in their comments? Do they appear fearful of making any suggestions and/or recommendations? Does this indicate that the organization is so top down and controlling that the assessment might not work too well in regard to its results being accepted? Look at Examples 4.3 and 4.4.

Example 4.3

Rigidness

Interviews were conducted in a large corporation with a small number of staff members about the nature and quality of organizational training. During the informal conversations the external assessors observed that the interviewees were not open to questions and would not provide much insight or information without heavy prompting. This standoffishness suggested that everything was not right in the setting. Constant reassurances had to be given as to the anonymous reports that would be made to the higher-up administrators.

(Continued)

(Continued)

Using other techniques, the external assessors were able to learn a good deal more about the organization and to verify their initial perceptions. The organization was uptight and very much top down. That information led to implementing a very successful program evaluation that uncovered a major training need. Without the initial observations it is doubtful that the work would have achieved the success that it did (Altschuld & Thomas, in press).

Example 4.4

Openness

A major and very large university department was examining its needs for curriculum and instructional reform. The chairperson of the department was an integral member of the team looking at possible changes. Being aware of group dynamics, the external facilitator was worried that its members (senior and junior faculty, some not tenured, and a graduate student) would be intimidated and not be willing to speak their minds especially when the chairperson offered ideas. Would they just acquiesce? Would they just go along?

If that was the case, then the likelihood of really looking at needs or discussing them would have been sharply diminished. If the observation held, the facilitator would have been wise to withdraw from the effort. Why work in an environment where program change or even conceptual adaptation is unlikely?

What the assessor saw led to continued persistence with the group. The discussion was lively with everybody's ideas open for challenge. The atmosphere encouraged by the chairperson was that in looking at needs everyone's ideas were equal. All group members were open to in-depth questioning and probing. This was a more exciting milieu and one that should lead to more meaningful needs.

The two contrasting examples bring the point home. Facilitators and NACs as participants in the assessment should be vigilant to the context as it originally was and as it changes over time. Usually this comes through unobtrusive observations and also the cultural audit. Aside from these there are other uses of observations in Phase I.

Look at services provided in programs and note if there are patterns of use and/or nonuse. Do materials and handouts in schools appear to be used? Are they dog eared and beat up? Are mental health facilities located in areas easily accessible especially to the populations they serve, if potential clients do not have independent means of transportation? If you are reviewing organizational communications, to whom are memos going, who is on the distribution list, who gets "carbon copied," and so forth? What happens in group discussions especially if certain individuals are present or not present?

One final situation comes to mind. In the experience of one of the authors, there was an instance where telltale signs of a political stand-off in the NAC made work by the group impossible. After examining a long-standing conflict in an initial meeting, the likelihood of success with the study seemed dismal. The two sides of the issue had marshaled their forces to such an extent that progress on the assessment seemed impossible. What happened then seems totally illogical, but for some reason, it worked.

- The needs assessor never called another meeting.

- The two sides were happy to avoid a conflict that was not settled satisfactorily until at least 2 years later by an administrative council vote.

- Apparently, the administrator who began the study (in this case, a university dean) had enough other concerns on his mind that he never raised another word about the proposed study. It seemed that he forgot about it, too.

In this instance inactivity (lethargy) paid off handsomely. (We cannot guarantee that similar results will occur another time!) Taking cues from initial information is vital to the success or failure of needs assessments. A combination of understanding and "gut feel" is important. Implicit aspects of a situation that mostly go unexpressed may provide a key to successful assessment. (Trust those feelings, "instincts.")

❖ CREATING DATA

Besides using existing sources, it may be desirable to create some new Phase I data. Some such as informal interviews are obvious, while others may not be immediately apparent such as focus groups.

The idea of informal interviews has been noted previously, so only a little will be added to what you already know. Formulate a few questions and set up a scheduled conversation or insert the questions during ongoing conversations. What we haven't mentioned before is who should be interviewed. It is fair to say that some people are more observant or more able to represent their point of view than others. One of the authors had an ongoing project developing qualitative reports about a federal government's funded project in "comprehensive child development," working with entire families admitted to the program. A project staff member showed an uncanny ability to see emerging trends and to comment on the project's progress. Discussions with this person established her as a "key informant." The insights gained saved inordinate amounts of time in locating detailed information. She possessed a better grasp of the project's intricacies than anyone else. Such a person can provide valuable insight from an insider's perspective, when trust is there.

If an assessment includes three or four people who are noticed to be consistently and independently uncomfortable with certain questions, this indicates sensitive, taboo areas and points toward some deep-seated issues that cannot be addressed in this assessment. The facilitator and the NAC should pause in thinking about what to do since meaningful change may not be possible in the situation.

❖ A POTPOURRI OF OTHER CONSIDERATIONS

These procedures can provide valuable data early in the assessment. Focus group procedures are popular. They require that you (a) convene a group, members of which have similar characteristics (e.g., all are beginning employees in a firm); (b) pose questions that catch members' attention and that tap into their realm of knowledge; (c) have one person asking the questions and another person recording; (d) use recording as a check for the completeness and accuracy of the results; and (e) write up findings in a narrative fashion.

In a recent study where focus groups were used, the number of persons invited to the focus group was between 10 and 15 people. Recognizing that scheduling conflicts often reduce these numbers, we were willing to proceed with the discussion if at least 5 persons attended (in one case, the number dropped to 2, but the quality of responses remained high, so the results were used). In the beginning of a needs assessment, one or two focus groups could provide a wealth of information. Figures 4.1 and 4.2 contain a general description of the procedures that were followed in the study just noted and the questions that were given out as a precursor to the interview. The goal was to learn about teacher attrition from those now in the teaching profession.

The difference between a focus group in Phase I and one in Phase II is in how much depth is covered by the questions and how many focus group sessions are conducted. It all depends on the needs being investigated. One other interesting use of a Phase I focus group might be to

Figure 4.1   In-Service Educator Focus Group Guide

Establish rapport with members of the group before beginning.

Main question: We're here to talk about the retention of teachers in our public schools; what are your thoughts on this subject?

Probes: During the discussion, watch for and bring up if necessary the following subjects:

No Child Left Behind legislation at the federal level

What keeps teachers focused and coming to work every day?

Perception of the teaching climate and culture in the state

Career ladder/professional development requirements and/or changes

Gender issues

What incentives might attract and retain high-quality teachers?

Concerns about the environment around their teaching position in terms of administration, collegial relations, facilities, students, parents, etc.

Support from fellow teachers, administrators, parents, staff, etc.

Conclude in one of two ways:

By summarizing what you've heard and asking for corrections or additional comments

By asking if there is anything else anyone wanted to say and didn't (and then going once more around the circle of participants for comments)

Figure 4.2   Pre–Focus Group Survey Used in the Teacher Supply Study

Initial Questionnaire for Preservice Focus Group Participants:

Welcome to this focus group organized by the Educator Supply and Demand Study. The work is being done under contract with the State Department of Education. Please respond candidly to the questions on this survey as well as in the focus group interview. In both the written and verbal feedback you provide, the information will be treated as anonymous data, reported in a way that can in no way be traced back to you as an individual. Thank you for your participation in the study.

Please respond to the questions below:

1. What grade/subject are you preparing to teach?
2. What factors have attracted you to an education major?
3. How long do you anticipate staying in the teaching profession?
4. What kind of support do you think you will receive when you begin teaching (administrative, mentoring, professional development, etc.)?
5. In what state are you planning to seek a teaching position?
6. What are your long-term career goals?

scout out and identify what should be probed much more in Phase II. This is an extension of what is often done in initial interviews and then subsequent ones in qualitative research. You develop hypotheses and issues that require more understanding and information later. It's a matter of degree, and in virtually all investigations revolving around needs, subtle decisions like these are commonly made.

The important distinction for a focus group in Phase I is simply to begin with a general but engaging question and to have a few backup questions in reserve if the initial one fails. In the teacher study, the stage was set with the initial questionnaire, and then discussion was launched by the question "We're here to talk about the retention of teachers in schools; what are your thoughts on the subject?"

That question is general, and the resulting discussion can go in myriad directions. The backup questions are more specific. For example, what keeps teachers coming to work every day? What incentives might attract and retain high-quality teachers? At this stage, exploring the terrain is important, but if the main question gets a short answer or silence, it is better to move to a more specific level and keep the discussion moving than to shut down the meeting too soon.

Another technique employed in Phase I is where selected persons receive and fill out a questionnaire and then, after the results have been tabulated, receive and fill out the same questionnaire while viewing the tabulated results from the group. This is a version of the traditional "Delphi" survey. In this age of rapid e-mail correspondence, surveying through one or two iterations could provide valuable data. This might be done with a few carefully worded open-ended questions or a small set of closed-ended ones to explore the issue with the members of the group (see Hung, Altschuld, & Lee, 2008).

Going even further a unique approach to creating data has been titled a "Community Speak-Up." This process takes somewhat longer to organize than to implement. A key individual who can address the overall issue under examination and many of its subissues is scheduled to speak in a public place, and the event is advertised. The person gives a short, informative speech, and then trained facilitators meet with members of the audience in groups of 10 to 15 for discussion sessions. The intent is to engage the community and get people energized about the topic.

Prior to discussion each person receives a set of about five 3 × 5" note cards and is asked to write his or her opinions of the topic on separate cards. After a few minutes of writing, the discussion begins. Participants are instructed that when any concern that they can relate to is mentioned, they are to write the concern with a statement of their opinion about it on a separate card. If they run out of cards, they receive additional ones as needed. After 30–45 minutes of discussion, when it feels like the topic has been fully explored (points are getting repeated), the facilitator concludes the discussion, thanks all for their input, and gathers the note cards.

Afterward, the cards are sorted into groups and content is analyzed with the number of persons noting a specific concern, and, qualitatively, particularly well-articulated statements that represent the essence of the expressed views are quoted. This procedure generates considerable data, especially if planned in advance and carried out well.

An offshoot of this procedure is to invite groups ($n = 10$–15) of selected stakeholders for small discussion sessions. Use short scenarios to kick off the exchange among the group. Frame a few opening questions and then get the individuals into thought-provoking positive exchanges of views. Record what comes up and then go through a summarizing process similar to that of the "Community Speak-Up."

This listing of potential approaches for data gathering is meant to be provocative, not exhaustive. In preparing to convene the NAC, be creative as you look at the literature and your particular assessment, and feel free to combine techniques or find ways to use them in as cost-effective a manner as you are able. They were offered as guidance and to whet your appetite for data collection and summarization in Phase I of the enterprise. See Example 4.5.

Example 4.5

Continuing With the Running Faculty Needs Assessment From Previous Chapters

In working with the departmental NAC and with the students who would do the data gathering, steps taken to build preliminary information were handled expeditiously.

1. Previous needs assessment reports were made available for review ($n = 2$) as was the report of an evaluation site visit by three prominent outsiders. Because some of the key players who had generated and used these reports were retiring, there was a bit of the feeling that "We are headed in a new direction, with new players. Let's not be hampered by past efforts; instead, let's set a new direction. The timing is right."

2. Because some new means of data gathering were envisioned, namely e-mail surveys, pilot testing would be required.

(Continued)

(Continued)

3. The final report was seen as important to pass along to future assessors. Little effort was made to maintain an audit trail, although with the ease of electronic data compilation, raw data were maintained.

4. For future assessments much preliminary work is now mandated by the Institutional Review Board, which includes approval of instruments and release forms for any photo or video taken. How this requirement would impact the kinds of preliminary data gathering espoused in this chapter is an open question. In our case we did not feel hampered by these procedures and did not concern ourselves with approval for pilot efforts (the e-mail questionnaire). Present requirements have become more restrictive.

5. Overall involvement of the NAC was rather low at this point, as the burden of work shifted to the graduate students. Thus the NAC was used more for consultation than for carrying out the work.

Highlights of the Chapter

1. Needs assessment is a seamless process that requires continual capitalizing on what has taken place from the start of the effort through to completion. The goal is to build upon what has been done before and to rely primarily upon available information.

2. To that end, the first key point was to see where the NAC is in the process and how what has been learned to date can be captured in a useable format for decision making and keeping an audit trail of the overall endeavor.

3. Several ways for summarizing data and information were offered with the admonition that all critical summaries (and tables) be dated.

4. Ways were suggested for collecting Phase I data with the notation that some of the methods might also fit Phase II but would be carried out in much greater depth at that time.

5. Possible decisions to be made in preassessment were explained.

6. Obtaining information from databases and prior reports (evaluations, prior needs assessments, etc.) was emphasized. That was followed by brief coverage of a set of other approaches and processes.

7. It was pointed out that these were just a sampling of things that could be done and the NAC should feel free to use others as they fit the specific setting.

8. The running example from prior chapters was continued.

5

The Special Case of Collaborative (Cooperative) Needs Assessments

As a rule, needs assessment is an activity performed by a single organization. Seldom do grassroots groups have the resources and expertise to do one. They may provide the impetus for an investigation, but it is the individual agency, business, or institution that usually conducts the process and implements solutions for identified problems.

Activities should be directed toward the needs of Level 1, service receivers, with those of Levels 2 and 3 being looked at down the road, as they are more related to resolving prioritized discrepancies. Needs assessment committees (NACs) that are formed to guide and direct the endeavor may have external members (including an external facilitator) and/or a representative range of stakeholders, but they primarily consist of individuals closely associated with the organization carrying out the study.

As a consequence the group may have an insulated point of view, only of the organization. While this may be good and the effort successful, tunnel vision and/or narrow group thinking might result. One organization may not have the wisdom and staff knowledge and skills to attend to, understand, devise, and put into play ways to alleviate the problems of the ultimate recipients of service.

What does this last statement really mean? Consider areas such as pollution, recreation, public health preparedness for natural disasters or terrorist attacks, poverty, issues related to senior citizens, the cost-effective delivery of health care, provision of high-quality educational programs, and others. Needs in these areas and dealing with underlying concerns are not the domain of one institution or organization. Air pollution does not stop at the borders of a state (unfortunately).

As another instance, when the horror of 9/11 struck us, what had to be brought to bear in terms of emergency assistance? Police, fire, and medical resources (emergency and longer-term) had to immediately appear and perform in unison on a scale they had not experienced before. Rescue teams, military personnel, specialized equipment, and groups of individuals came from all over the country. Beyond that, think about the food that had to be there for those individuals and groups on-site, the crews for removal of trash, the specially trained animals and their handlers that had to be located, the communication and coordination needs that had to be taken care of, and such entities as water, electric, and gas companies that had to be involved. Over and above the immediate problems, contemplate the emotional and health needs that arose for the emergency workers, a situation that still persists at the time of this writing many years later.

A corollary to what was just described and an even more complicated problem focuses on the heavy-duty equipment required to remove major ruins. Although New York City is one of the largest metropolitan areas in the world, there are limits to how much of this equipment can be there and accessible locally in a short period of time. What often happens is that it has to be brought from a distance with all the support necessary for the teams utilizing it. Other tragedies, whether natural or by human hand in sites around the globe, attest to the difficulties of situations like these.

An interesting assessment applicable to this situation is briefly described in Book 3 of this KIT. It is the "after action report," which can take several forms. In that book an interview procedure as used with service providers in the aftermath of Hurricane Katrina in New Orleans was described in some detail (Hites, 2006). Questions were of the following type, among others:

- What kinds of things did you run into for which you were not prepared or trained?

- What kinds of support would have helped you most?

- What is your current emotional and physical state?

An almost retrospective look at needs like this, while traumatic and trying for both assessors and respondents, might lead to some highly utilitarian findings. It would illuminate problems that assistance providers encountered, their perceptions of the adequacy of their training, and a very intense personal view of a sad situation.

The same type of collaborative environment would be apparent in the tsunami tragedy in Indonesia and surrounding countries (and subsequent worldwide aid) and the earthquakes experienced in Turkey, Yugoslavia, Pakistan, and elsewhere after that. The need for collaboration, cooperative services, and a different frame for defining the investigation of needs is immediately apparent.

❖ COLLABORATION AND COOPERATION

It is worthwhile to differentiate between the terms *collaborative* and *cooperative*. The distinction is one more of degree (although it can be sizeable) than of kind. Collaboration implies partnership with shared decision making and a sense of ownership, strong communication, and full participation in the collective endeavor as one end of a continuum. The concept relies on a high amount of trust among the parties (organizations and their appointed representatives) providing services and those receiving them. It means willingness to cede some part of one's turf with the recognition that something is given up for the greater good and more will be accomplished this way. In theory this sounds great, but in practice it is hard to achieve.

The opposite pole (the cooperative one) is where there is participation but not *full* participation. For example, a needs assessment may require that an agency be asked to help with supplying or collecting information, but other than that, it is not playing a major role in the process. It is cooperating but not collaborating. It contributes to the enterprise and possibly to solution strategies but to a much lesser extent than in collaboration.

Aside from disaster situations, there are many positive circumstances where it would be beneficial for organizations to collaborate in terms of a mutual exploration of needs and in working together to improve or completely remove gaps. One field in which this would readily apply is education.

In one author's home state there are far too many medical schools (a number of which were only established in the last 30–40 years) and teacher training postsecondary institutions. Regarding the medical schools, they are more numerous than would be justified based on comparisons to other similar states in terms of population.

Even though some of the institutions are not publicly supported, in the end it is the taxpayer who pays for most of the duplication. Some overlap is fine, but when excessive it is not. There are analogous issues in this same state related to how many persons are being trained in medical technology, dental hygiene, and related fields.

With the little p word (politics) rearing its head (why had such programs and institutions been funded in the first place?), it would seem to have been better if collaborative needs assessments and in turn a better job of planning, funding, and implementing programs in accordance with the results had been done. Given vested local interests that now have arisen for the medical programs, it would be difficult to change or seriously affect the present configuration in the state. To change at this time would create another problem and a serious one in and of itself.

❖ PROS AND CONS OF COLLABORATIVE
NEEDS ASSESSMENTS

In line with the above comments, what are some positives and negatives for the idea of collaboration (or at least getting more cooperation in the process)? Table 5.1 contains a sampling of those reasons.

Table 5.1   A Sampling of Reasons For and Against Collaborative Needs
Assessments

For	Against
Shared resources lead to economies of scale for the needs assessment and action plans to resolve underlying discrepancies	Fear of loss of turf or control of one's situation
Money saved could be used for new and/or additional services	Unless the assessment is set up in an equitable manner there could be acrimony The ill will may offset any monetary and/or other gains

For	Against
Better use of staff skills in organizations and not having to duplicate all types of work	Limited exposure to or experience in working collaboratively across institutions
Not having to operate in a competitive environment	Sometimes plans developed by committees and/or across institutions will not be very good The old idea that it looks like the product of a committee (with negative connotations)
Improvement of available services that are poorly delivered at the present time	It will be difficult to sustain a needs assessment and an action plan evolving from it when many parties are involved
Cross-organizational fertilization of ideas	Larger entities may inadvertently or even openly dominate the collective (lack of parity coupled with a fear of being overwhelmed)
Creating opportunities and in turn new job possibilities Collective actions could lead to new avenues of response	Elimination of jobs and reductions in force (job insecurity) This could affect the willingness of staff to openly give their input and opinions during the assessment process
Positive effects of cross-organizational communication	The normal competitive spirit will emerge
New experiences, meeting new people, new ideas, stimulating growth and change	Way too much hassle and not worth the effort

It is obvious that there are nearly the same number of pros and negatives. In needs assessment classes, we have used an environment mapping activity (described subsequently) and asked students after they have completed the basic map to think about reasons for and opposed to working together. They were encouraged to be creative in their thinking. When their responses were listed on the board, it was not surprising that the two sides were nearly equal.

Collaborations require more time and subtlety than meets the eye, and in many cases they simply have not worked. When the students were further pushed to come up with strategies for strengthening those forces that make for success, they posited some rather interesting ideas. Among them are to obtain

- an external coordinator to start the process so as to minimize conflicts and facilitate groups working with each other;

- testimonials from others who have been part of successful such ventures (benchmarking would be useful and provide guidance); and

- approval for convening at least one meeting of the collaborative group in Aruba, Hawaii, or a similar location more suitable to reaching consensus for next steps, a tongue-in-cheek suggestion but, nevertheless, the most intriguing (note Figure 5.3).

Before moving into whether an organization should look into forming a collaborative, there are a few other guiding principles for such collective work. They generally come from our experience in the field.

❖ SOME PRINCIPLES FOR WORKING TOGETHER

First, working in a collaborative or a cooperative environment takes more time. More views enter into plans, assessments, evaluations, implementations of activities, and so on with the ultimate effect of slowing things down. Take, for example, an evaluation where an evaluator or a team of evaluators would present draft instruments for consideration of a committee comprising various partners in a consortium. One could imagine how meetings would quickly degenerate if the wording of each survey item were to be dissected and amended by consensus. So the trick would be to gain input that is reasonable and timely yet allows work to get done on a meaningful schedule.

One way to do this would be to describe the rationale underlying the evaluation and the instruments and, following some discussion about the approach, to ask that suggestions and changes be sent to the developers later. The goal is not to close off ideas and new directions but to have a mechanism for doing so in a manner that does not slow activities to a crawl (see White & Altschuld, 2009, and White, Altschuld, & Lee, 2008, for a more in-depth discussion of how this was achieved in a 15-university statewide consortium!).

Second, a factor relevant to a number of entries in Table 5.1 is the idea of "turf." The need to control what one does or to have control of what one's organization would be doing is prominent with potentially a disastrous impact on the success of a collaborative effort. This control issue will be especially evident in assessments when values are discussed. How is this problem circumvented?

Originally, and in a naïve vein, one of the authors thought that rotating the leadership of a collaborative NAC would lead to a greater sense of ownership and shared communication, similar to the way that the presidency of the European Union is rotated. The flaw in this ploy is that it just doesn't work in many cases. Central and continuing leadership will do more to enhance working together for mutual benefit, especially if issues or finer points are attended to and resolved in a timely manner.

The facilitator of the collective endeavor faces quite a challenge in setting a tone for how the group will function. Recognizing the need to periodically summarize and then to move ahead, the group will probably have to work on needs that are relatively important for all organizations but not necessarily the top concern for any one institution. An environment must be established where all organizations and their representatives on the NAC feel that they are involved in the process and part of the approval mechanism for solution strategies to eliminate needs. This type of mind-set should occur as much as possible for all deliberations and work of the group.

A fun way to reinforce the attitude that we are all in this together is to alternate where NAC meetings are held. Different groups playing host change the pace and dimensions of what is going on in a very positive manner. Be open to ways that enhance the sense of participation in the collective.

The third point is to make sure that the focus of the group's work will be of enough interest to all and will capture their imagination. If you as the leader have a good sense of what might motivate the NAC early in the collaboration, quickly review some literature and send out a readable and fitting article or two to spark discussion and thinking. This activity is fruitful and does get group members to express ideas and perceptions of problems. People like to see how their particular circumstance ties into the larger picture.

The fourth consideration is that it is valuable for the facilitator to have had experience in cross-organizational programs and, better yet, in cross-organizational needs assessments. It takes a great deal of patience to lead a collaborative assessment—a lot more than one internal to an organization (this is not intended to minimize the effort required for an internal examination of needs). The concepts involved in investigating needs are much the same whether it is internal or a collaborative, more expansive endeavor, but in the latter the leader has to be sensitive to the politics of each group that is participating. There is no substitute for experience—knowing when to press ahead and when to return to prior points, learning about contacts in multiple organizations, and so forth. A sense of the collective good, that we are in this together for our mutual benefit, helps as well.

The fifth principle may appear somewhat down the road in the assessment game. It deals with problem resolution. Given that multiple needs might occur, view the collective like a large NAC with more resources at its disposal. Consider having subgroups of members write proposals for resources that wind up benefiting the collective while at the same time being housed in a location apart from the lead organization. This could lead to local and collective advantages, a win-win proposition.

The last point here deals with patience. In most needs assessments there is an imperative, an urgency to move ahead at a rapid pace. At early meetings of the NAC (consisting of representatives of member organizations), stress that everyone should recognize that it will take time for the collective endeavor and vision to materialize and that is a common occurrence across entities like these. Periodically remind members of the NAC not only of progress but also of the necessity of taking the long view.

❖ CHOOSING COLLABORATING ORGANIZATIONS

How do collaborative needs assessments start? The facilitator and the NAC perceive that they cannot deal with the needs (even though they haven't done a formal assessment at this point) by themselves. The problems are too big and require the involvement of others.

In seeking collaborators to assess needs, it is prudent to look carefully at the environment of an organization and visually and conceptually map that landscape. This is like a technique (rapid rural appraisal) used in countries where not highly literate populations create maps of community resources. An analogous procedure comes from the work of Lauffer (1982). He developed the basic concept from his background in community development around the world.

The key premise is that many problems in social welfare, education, health, and other areas inherently cut across organizations and cannot be improved unless there is some form of collaboration. (Note: This approach might be more difficult to apply in competitive business settings where market share protection is a paramount issue.)

The process starts by describing what the organization is, what service it provides, and how it relates to other organizations and groups that are receivers of its services or products or that provide input to it so it can deliver same. The process is analytical and makes participants think deeply about how their organization and their part of the local situation relate to a larger, more complex social structure. They are encouraged to think broadly even to considering relationships that don't currently exist but perhaps should.

Then they embark on the activity as shown below (see Figure 5.1 for the structure of the environment map). The steps to create the map provide a sense of what might be involved in collaboration. At this stage the process is internal to one organization, but as time progresses it could easily become external. The map will tend to pinpoint or suggest which prime individuals or groups might be included later.

Figure 5.1   Organizational Environment Map

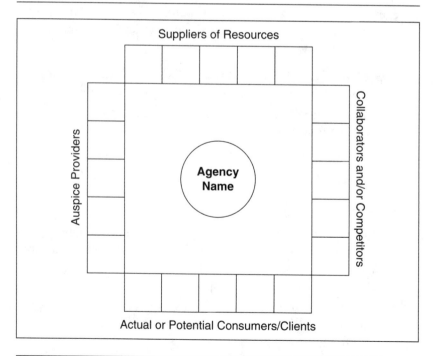

Source: Adapted from Lauffer (1982). Used by permission of Sage Publications.

Step 1. Describe in a short paragraph or two the mission of the organization, its Level 1 constituency, and the basic services or products it delivers. Keep the description brief and focused.

By being direct and short, participants are forced to say, "This, in a nutshell, is what we are about and what we do. This is what we stand for and what is important to us." It takes some contemplation to do this, but it is worthwhile.

Step 2. Complete the Lauffer (1982) type chart by adding those elements for clients with whom the organization interacts or should interact in the ideal world. In other words, this introspection may reveal serious gaps in communication with others or linkages that are not there.

The general categories are on the outside edges of the map. They include collaborators and competitors, auspice providers (those who give the sanction for the organization to exist—government, laws, boards, etc.), and other categories (see boxes on the outer sides of the map). If you feel that there should be categories different from Lauffer's (1982), adapt the procedure to your situation.

(It might be best if each NAC member did this and then the total committee synthesized individual perceptions. We often do this with numerous techniques to avoid the emergence of a more limiting groupthink.)

Step 3. Next the goal is to identify how the organization does or does not relate to what has been identified for each of the categories.

- Does a linkage between the organization and the boxes on the outside currently exist?
- How strong is that linkage?
- Should it exist?
- How important is such linkage for determining and resolving problems or needs?
- How amenable would our organization and others be to a collaborative needs assessment and to coming together to resolve needs?

In the original format for the activity the NAC would seek agreement as to how strong the linkages are or should be, whether or not they are critical to eventual identification and rectification of needs, and so on.

When this activity has been used in classes, the latter parts of Step 3 have not seemed as meaningful as was intended. Instead what works better is that now the group is primed for quickly saying, "These are the most influential outside entities to become part of our needs assessment." A Pareto-type principle applies in that if many organizations are listed, only a small set will be candidates for participating in the assessment.

Step 4. This is where the activity takes an interesting twist. What does the group think are the forces that would propel others to join with it, and what are those that would be negative in this regard?

> "This is our needs assessment, so why would anyone want to join with us in this journey? Why should they invest their time, energy, and resources to work on this? Sure, they might want to help us, but what about fully collaborating? What's in it for them and their organization?"

These questions will arise and have to be dealt with before approaching potential collaborators.

Step 5. A way to engage the group is by expanding on Step 4. What are we offering for those whose involvement we seek? Certainly ideas arising from the work on Figure 5.1 should be percolating through the committee. Is there some way we could strengthen the forces for collaboration and reduce those that work against resolving needs with others, in a fashion similar to a force field analysis (Figure 5.2)?

It shows the "helping" and "hindering" forces. Usually this is done by brainstorming all kinds of forces irrespective of whether they are positive or negative. Then they are grouped, and via discussion they are deemed as factors that work in favor of a proposition or against it. Eventually, if the group so decides, they can be placed on a force field diagram and their strengths can be estimated. What is not obvious is how to reduce the strength of the hindering forces or strengthen those that are helpful.

How to deal with many of the factors brought up so far depends on the local context and conditions. The internal group is a good sounding board for the options. More elaborate force field analyses using graphic arrows to show strength of forces or numerical rankings to calculate strength or weakness are given in Rothwell, Hohne, and King (2007).

Figure 5.2   Generic Diagram for Force Field Analysis: Driving and
Restraining Forces

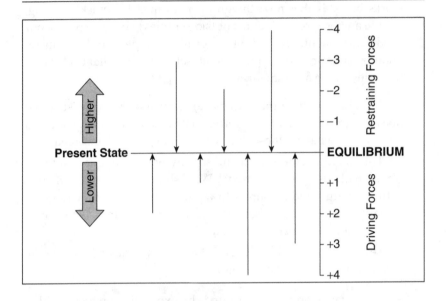

Ask members of the committee to consider why others don't join in or participate. Challenge their imagination. Everyone who has worked for a period of time in organizations, agencies, and businesses has seen collaborative arrangements fail and has horror stories about them! Retrospectively, what has made them work well, and what have been shortcomings? Be open about this because the negative factors are strong! What seems to work for success, and/or how could we turn the negatives into positives?

This activity has been very effective in sensitizing people to the precariousness of a seemingly simple proposition. It has worked for practitioners in numerous workshops we have conducted and in our classes. In our experience there are fewer collaborative and cooperative endeavors than would be expected given the complexity of many problems confronting societies and communities as noted previously. The maintenance or control of one's own turf involves much more powerful (dominant) forces than often perceived and stands rather prominently in the way of combining resources to assess needs and ameliorate problems. A line from the Rodgers and Hammerstein musical, *The King and I,* stands out: "If allies are strong with power to protect me, why they not protect me out of all I own?" Perhaps the activity has too much of a central planning feel to it and turns off some individuals.

Lest the perception remain that this cooperative work is a nice academic exercise but not one very useful in the real world, let us dispel such doubts. The majority of the students we teach are older (average age would be above 35) and are pursuing graduate education after many years of teaching, delivering health care services, working with social programs, administering programs, and doing related activities. They have professional, real-world experience and are acutely aware of many of the difficulties that groups and organizations encounter when they try working together, and hence that background may account for the nearly equal loading of positive and negative forces. They enjoy the mapping activity and feel it fits situations they have seen before. The composition of NACs will generally be similar to that of the classes, and the technique should function much as described.

(To see suggestions and what students came up with, note Figure 5.3, which is an abbreviated form of what resulted from their deliberations. There are some cultural slants to their perspectives as most of them were American and Caucasian. Despite that fact, much of what they felt might be in play in the collaborative situation would seem to generalize across cultural boundaries.)

Figure 5.3   A Sampling of Reasons For and Against Collaboration and Ways to Strengthen Collaboration Generated by Classes of Students Over Time

---

Reasons For:

- Greater understanding of others
- Exchange of knowledge and information
- Efficiency of financial expenditures
- Providing new services (ones not previously available)
- Expanding services currently being delivered
- Cross-training of staff (e.g., via in-service programs)
- Increase in communication
- Being able to exert more political clout
- Greater public visibility
- Enhancing legitimacy of efforts
- Gaining a competitive edge
- A host of other entries

(Continued)

Figure 5.3 (Continued)

Reasons Against:

- Tradition; why change?
- Turf issues (control and competition)
- Why share when we already have a lot?
- Personalities
- American way (lack of cooperation), which may only be applicable to one or similar cultures
- Fear of failure
- Different agency funding sources and therefore budgetary constraints
- Time pressures
- Basic organization constituencies that are too different
- Lack of institutional history and knowledge in collaboration/cooperation
- Disputes over responsibilities
- Many more

Ways to Strengthen:

- Look for common goals while watching out for conflicts
- Bring in outsiders to provide testimonials
- Jointly seek a variety of resources that could be combined
- Emphasize the strengths of the arguments that would be supportive of collaboration
- Build on established communication and other networks
- Use an outside and impartial coordinator to head the effort
- Find short-term needs where you can have immediate or rapid success
- Have your meetings and sessions in Aruba, Puerto Rico, Hawaii, etc.

As the mapping exercise and discussion winds down, the facilitator of the NAC should gently guide the group toward a decision. Make the choice wisely and with clear understanding of what it entails.

- Are we of the mind that we should solicit others (collaborators or cooperators) to enter into our needs assessment?

- How many such groups could we invite and still have a feasible assessment?

- What are the advantages for us? For them?

- What could these other groups contribute to the investigation of needs and, later, solution strategies?

- What are the disadvantages (to us), and do they outweigh the benefits?

- How should we approach others—what should we emphasize on why this should appeal to them?

- Who should be responsible for taking the lead in doing this, and at what level of the organizations should it take place?

- What might be our thinking if we have to compromise in terms of needs that are important to us but may not be our highest priorities?

- How ready is our organization to go into such a mode of operating?

- Can timelines be expanded to accommodate the requirements of a collaborative?

- Does our organization have any small seed funds that could be applied to starting the collaborative or at least the first few organizational meetings?

Much comes from collaboration, but gains could be along a rocky path and will not occur without effort and dedication to making a meaningful, joint venture that is successful.

To further illustrate many of the ideas we have presented, consider Example 5.1. It comes from a statewide project designed to promote collaboration across universities to help in attracting to science, technology, engineering, and mathematics (STEM) underrepresented minority students and to retain their numbers through to graduation in relevant fields. Anyone who has worked in higher education will immediately recognize the turf issue, especially in states with duplication of educational programs. How then could the group of universities move forward?

Example 5.1

A Collaborative Insight!

The consortium was statewide with most of the main private and public universities taking part in it. It began quite slowly with meetings periodically at the lead institution in the state. A steering committee of university representatives (mostly minority faculty members or administrators) was formed, and it essentially became the oversight and implementation mechanism for the consortium.

One of the authors served as a member of the committee and the statewide evaluator. From his perspective, trust was going to be a precious commodity that would only come about over a great deal of time.

(Continued)

(Continued)

Although there was not a formal needs assessment, the consortium administrator was in frequent communication with the universities asking them to think about needs and activities to be undertaken in that regard as events progressed. Lots of concerns were debated, and little was evident other than a group beginning to form and establish some infrastructure. Somewhat into the second year some seminal ideas began to appear that could energize the collective activities of the group and create exciting positive momentum.

One was to establish a statewide research forum in which undergraduate students prepare posters and make presentations as though they are at a professional meeting. This event has slowly become an annual, well-attended function in the state and helps fulfill the need for acculturating students to professional life. No individual institution could easily carry this out on its own. The forum was focused on a feature that was missing (a gap, if you will) in undergraduate STEM education, and it was the galvanizing element in showing what collaboration might accomplish. The outcomes of this event helped reinforce the collective identity.

Moreover, several of the yearly forums have been held at locations other than the lead institution. This shift of venue underscores that the collaborative is truly embracing all schools rather than being dominated by one member or at least that the impression of hegemony has been seriously diminished.

One other thing was done in the same mode. A need that was discussed was that students can major in, say, chemistry or engineering anywhere in the state but may not be able to look at specialties such as polymer chemistry or robotics at their home university. With minimal funds allocated through the consortium and with some from their own institution, an exchange program was begun in the summer whereby students would study for 6–8 weeks at another university. This has proved to be popular, and indeed many of the student presentations and posters at the forum are derived from experiences on campuses away from home. Evaluations of the forum and the resulting mentoring have been positive for students and faculty participants.

In this consortium a base has been built, upon which future collaboration is now possible, not just for the program but also for evaluation. Everybody is part of what has been going on and hopefully will continue, a stance extended even to the evaluation team members. The evaluators have been asked to become involved in three related endeavors being done on other campuses in the state. This kind of collaborative experience is not a common occurrence.

This is not to say that all was smooth sailing, but a sense of teamwork, which is so difficult to achieve, had been realized. Now the task is to be vigilant to keep using the camaraderie and accomplishments to everyone's collective advantage.

Other observations about the example are pertinent. At the time of this writing, the 15 universities in the consortium have been working together for over 5 years (not a small accomplishment given the issues related to controlling one's space). During this period, the membership from some of the campuses has shifted and changed, making it a bit more difficult to maintain organizational memory and a consistent stance. A facilitator of such a group has to be vigilant in regard to keeping it and particularly its newer members on the same page. And, of all things, the facilitator also has changed. Lastly, note that not all members of the committee are at the same level or status. That has not caused any problems in the current situation, but it could in others. The facilitator has to be alert to this possibility and, if it is there, act to maintain the involvement of all players on as equal a basis as feasible.

Before moving to other aspects of collaboration, Belle Ruth Witkin (a mentor for both of us) wrote extensively about a collaborative assessment that she facilitated (Witkin, 1984). Four major groups were carefully chosen with attention to principles of inclusion and communication. The assessment utilized multiple methods extensively, the resulting data were integrated, and appropriate findings were drawn.

Without going into all of the gory details, the effort was almost a total failure. There are many pitfalls and traps along the way to prevent having a meaningful consortium—one that goes well beyond what any individual member could do and one in which all have a sense of truly shared ownership. Many of the preceding ideas were based on Witkin's (1984) analysis of what went wrong and why. Hopefully her catastrophe can help us avoid repeating such mistakes.

Additionally the work of Fiorentine (1993) would be useful here for understanding principles, particularly political ones, regarding the distribution of financial resources for needs (although, in Example 5.1, such resources were very scarce and over time the consortium members became adept at pooling them to have a much larger-than-expected impact). We encourage you to look at the literature for guidance on the nuances of collaborative needs assessments. When they work in an equitable and efficient manner, it is clearly the way to go. Generally, it takes more time than anticipated to get movement in the right direction. If working together does not gel, such a project can be quite disadvantageous and really sap enthusiasm and energy. *Enter into it with optimism and hope, but take care and have patience!*

❖ SOME OTHER COLLABORATION CONSIDERATIONS

There are other factors in collaboration that might have to be thought about depending on specific local conditions and the nature of the organizations involved or whose involvement might be sought. Several of these will be briefly explained.

Bilateral and multilateral endeavors. It is one thing to have two collaborating organizations (bilateral) and quite another to have three or more (multilateral). There are greater resources available in larger collaborations but more hassles ranging from the mundane, such as how to organize and schedule meetings and where to have them, to the subtle (giving up control) and eventually to the ultimate selection and prioritization of need areas to be resolved. Remember that all of this work has to be done through the filters of multiple organizations (staffs, administrators), the Level 1 constituencies they serve (which may or may not be the same or overlap to varying degrees), and their willingness to commit resources to the collective effort.

Within and across sectors. Collaborations could be thought of as being within the public sector (educational institutions working together to look at mutual needs), within the private sector (companies working together to reduce the costs of coming up with hybrid technology for more fuel-efficient automobiles), or across sectors (public and private groups working in unison in regard to public health preparedness for disasters). There are complexities to consider in each of these including hierarchy within a sector (a large educational institution overshadowing a small one), distrust, not being sure of relationships (private companies and government organizations), and proprietary concerns (companies not willing to share ideas for fear of losing their business and market share). Governance and communication with consortia-like arrangements must be sensitive to issues, overt or hidden, as just provided.

Whose needs and priorities? Different organizations will most likely have related yet distinct constituencies at the same time. This will also be true of their purposes and the services they provide. How do committees composed of their representatives decide which of the needs will be of highest priority for them to offer resources, time, staff, and support? For example, one hospital may focus on a less well-off population whereas another may be dealing with a better-financed group of patients.

Needs selection for attention. A good general rule to follow would be to select a need(s) that is (are) of fairly high importance for all involved organizations with the recognition that it may not be the highest for any one of them. Compromise would be the order of the day. Whichever need is chosen, it must have a modicum of appeal to each of the participating groups.

High-visibility needs that can be quickly resolved. Collaborations are fragile entities. They are not just hard to get started; they are more difficult to sustain. Indeed some of the forces against this type of interaction and problem identification/resolution are very strong.

With that in mind and with the old admonition that success breeds success, choose needs that can be solved fairly fast and that have high visibility. Doing so should reinforce the idea that the collaborative can accomplish more than individual members.

Governance. When groups begin to work together, a need arises as to how the collective should function and be structured so that it goes beyond the communication and the trading off of ideas (those activities are good, but by themselves insufficient for resolving needs). One suggestion for governing such arrangements that you might think about (that we argued against earlier) would be to have leadership within the group rotate on a regular basis. This would tend to reduce the fear of domination and at the same time enhance the feeling of involvement and ownership of all groups and participants. Note: We are talking here about rotating the leadership of a long-term (multiyear) effort, not a single-instance needs assessment study.

In the STEM project previously depicted, it was not feasible to do this since there was a central administrator at the lead institution. So rotating leadership may not work as well as one would hope. But a semblance of this idea could do a lot for perceptions of full and more even engagement. It took some time in the STEM partnership to work out such arrangements. Not only did two of the other institutions host the annual statewide research forum; several smaller training sessions conducted at universities other than the main one were also implemented.

Little things like this can go a long way in promoting the idea that everyone is in the same boat. Other universities became willing to offer their locations for consortium activities. (For a historical example of such compromises, look at how the two houses of the U.S. Congress, the Senate and House of Representatives, are balanced in their selection of members to accommodate large and small states.)

Who should be in the leadership group? The whole idea of collaboration is tricky, and a good part of the ultimate success or failure will come from leadership of the collaboration and the commitment that can be engendered by this group of individuals. It would be helpful if representatives were in high-level roles in their organizations and/or were influential in terms of how decisions get made at home.

They would be attuned to how their organizations operate, how resources are allocated, internal politics, and so on. They may not be formal leaders, but they have the ear of those who are and/or are sought out for wise advice and counsel. Every organization has this type of person, and they can make the collaborative an effective and positive mechanism for change.

At the same time, there can be unevenness in the membership of NACs and/or steering committees. And, as noted, some members will leave, and new representatives come aboard. Consistency in the group is desirable as group history is developed. Recently one of the authors indicated a willingness to orient a new committee member for a nationwide committee he was chairing, but the individual did not favorably respond and indeed was criticizing prior actions when he first participated. Being critical is not the issue, but doing so in the absence of why prior actions were taken is not good. The wise facilitator should suggest orientation via continuing members. We think that this would reduce or eliminate problems such as just described.

Beyond consistency there may be power or status dimensions on the committee. The facilitator should be aware of these and operate along the lines of a focus group interview. Call on different individuals to voice their opinions and make sure that power disparities are kept to as much of a minimum as possible. Over time they tend to ameliorate when members see their ideas incorporated into collaborative activities.

❖ THE RUNNING EXAMPLE FROM PREVIOUS CHAPTERS

It is fair to say that, in a university department setting like the one in the earlier chapters, a joint needs assessment would only make sense if there was a good rationale and where the value of some sort of combination of resources and purposes emerged. Combinations are frequently proposed (Instructional Technology, the academic department, merging with campus services like video production, graphic services, and information technology services). Though this may make pragmatic and philosophical sense for some (involving graduate students in helping conduct the work of the campus as they are studying about it), the department has a long history of resisting such moves, because its academic mission has been seen as of utmost importance.

Often other kinds of organizational mergers are espoused in the name of efficiency. Because the department, unlike others on campus, has no undergraduate major and concentrates on (more expensive) master's and doctoral work, such proposals come up with regularity. So far, in the 35 years of the department's existence, they have been avoided. That is not true of similar departments at other peer or referent institutions.

The downside of a collaborative assessment in this case would be diminished power for accreditation purposes, being more general than specific. Thus the actual study did not involve other units, but it did receive assistance from the Office of Analysis, Assessment, and Accreditation on campus, especially in regard to displaying results on the Web. But combining with another entity to conduct the effort was not considered seriously. The results are available on the Web at http://itls.usu.edu/files/Final%20Report%202004.pdf. (DeMars et al., 2004a)

Also keep in mind that the context was that of a single department and collaborative work for it simply did not and probably would not fit. Conversely, as departments in sometimes financially challenged institutions think about renewal and change, they may see it as beneficial to engage in collaborative examination of needs and their subsequent resolution. When that day comes, we encourage them to review concepts and ideas included in this chapter.

Highlights of the Chapter

1. There are many areas of need that cry out for a coordinated effort across institutions in terms of identification and prioritization of needs and then collectively resolving them. It was noted that such collaborations are less frequently observed in needs assessment than should be the case.

2. Given the above observation, reasons for and against working together were suggested.

3. An activity for mapping the environment of the organization was described, as was its use in pointing toward what other organizations might join in and what might be the rationale for getting involved.

4. Force field analysis was briefly mentioned in the context of Point 3. It illustrates the versatility of procedures and how they can be applied in combination to produce a better outcome.

5. Other principles for collaborative endeavor were explained. Every situation and circumstance is different, so apply them as fitting local parameters. Consortium work always requires much in the way of finesse.

6

Some of Those Nagging Leftover Pieces of Phase I

At this point in the needs assessment journey, you have a lot of ideas and strategies for conducting Phase I activities. But there still are many questions and unresolved issues about entering into an assessment. Now we have the opportunity to clear them up or at least to better inform you about the process. With that in mind, here are those leftovers.

❖ HOW MUCH TIME SHOULD BE ALLOTTED FOR PHASE I?

How much time is the phase going to take? This is difficult to answer, and it only was referred to in a general way earlier. If the assessment is for a smaller entity such as a department in a university of four or five faculty members, a retirement community of several hundred units, a rather focused and not very large area of a specialized center, and so on, the time will not be excessive. Perhaps a few months up to 6 would suffice with numerous meetings occurring at the beginning and somewhat less of them as progress is made.

Add in the type of need(s) being examined, and the time dimensions become clearer. It is not a gargantuan task to study the recreational and social needs of a retirement community or what could be a new focus or direction for an area within a center. These should not take much for preliminary exploration, at least in terms of Phase I.

It might be wise to discuss timelines with the NAC at one of its first meetings as issues are first being considered. Members are knowledgeable and able to provide input for the time and resources for the job. Even if these are off, ballpark estimates would be useful.

When needs are major and affect a lot of people and cut across many areas in an organization, then Phase I will take longer. For example, if you were to be looking at the entire center as it seeks funding or if the retirement community was quite big and diverse, the phase would be more complex. In Book 1 of the KIT a scenario was given for assessing needs for and then moving to action planning and implementation for a personnel evaluation system for over 400 employees spanning a range of occupations in a large college in a university. The basic work in that assessment lasted appropriately 6–7 months and continued in abated form for another 5.

The facilitator develops a reasonable and likely schedule, predicated upon his or her sense of the organization, what the needs assessment committee (NAC) suggests, the nature of the discrepancy, and other factors. It includes the number of meetings, how much time they will entail, and a possible set of tasks and procedures for keeping the effort focused and moving forward. Just in case the effort might be bigger than anticipated, plan for a few extra meetings. It is important to get all of the NAC to each small or large group session. The discussions and deliberations are vital, and all voices need to be heard.

Time is more problematic when the needs are of great import and cut across more constituencies and/or units in a company or an agency. More sessions and meetings will be mandatory over a contracted period. Similarly, if the needs assessment involves multiple sponsors/ participants, time will expand. In these instances the work of the facilitator is more demanding.

❖ WHO SHOULD LEAD THE GROUP?

Hidden in the heading are many subtle dimensions, some discussed or alluded to before. A larger, more complex assessment is usually led by an external individual who brings advantages to the enterprise. That individual tends to have the following skills:

- knowledge of methods and techniques;

- knowledge of how to organize an assessment;

- a repertoire of techniques for working with a NAC;

- prior experience using many (but not all) of the methods;

- no vested interests in the local situation;

- no historical baggage (at least not any related to this project!);

- the likelihood of being more dispassionate and objective since they are there only to assist the organization in assessing its needs;

- familiarity with the literature;

- some knowledge of where critical sources for Phase I might be found; and

- expertise and experience in leading previous assessments.

An external facilitator adds a "cachet" to the endeavor and may afford an opportunity for NAC members to state opinions and ideas that had not previously surfaced or had been kept from the public forum. On the other hand, such an individual will be more costly, and if a lot of time and extra work is required, the expense will be noticeable. And there are disadvantages to being external:

- not knowing local personalities and how to handle them;

- lack of understanding of where sources of influence are in the organization;

- having to become familiar with the organization in a short period of time (go back to the cultural audit in Chapter 2);

- needing more time to conduct and guide the study as a result of the prior point;

- the possibility that lack of in-depth and meaningful understanding of the organization could lead to a more superficial investigation;

- becoming a focal point (lightning rod) for past disagreements that arise as values enter into the process;

- being perceived as an outsider (not really sensing the locals and their needs);

- suspicion on the part of the staff that the individual is hired by administrators and represents a proadministrative stance;

- interrupted activity, being involved for a period of time and then leaving the scene as is normal for a consultant (no sustained, long-term participation);

- not investing in the results and subsequent changes (whereas members of the NAC know that they have to live with what happens in terms of policy, jobs, and even jobs being threatened, an altered work environment); and

- the use of precious resources to hire the person.

So what happens is that a hard choice is forced on the administration authorizing the assessment or the group advocating for it. Within it there are three basic concerns—costs, objectivity or an objective (neutral) stance, and knowledge and experience in doing this kind of work.

An internal person may be found who satisfies all three of the conditions and who would do as well as an outsider. In the ideal world, that internal individual may command equally the respect of the administration and staff. If so, the cost savings are substantial, and the likelihood of subsequent action may be greater since the facilitator knows how to get things done in the setting. The person would have a better perspective on stating and communicating findings, how to win support, or how to convince reluctant areas of the organization about the importance and urgency of needs. There are noticeable advantages to looking internally.

The phrasing "the ideal world" was intentional. The price for going internally may be too great in terms of vested interests and historical baggage. In the first book in this KIT, this was portrayed as a "penny-wise and pound foolish" decision. That example (6.1) as repeated below is an illustration of having to think about leadership for the assessment.

Example 6.1

Don't Be Pennywise but Pound Foolish!

A public service organization, which receives its financial support from both state and federal sources, was undergoing cutbacks in funding. At the same time it was subject to rapidly changing demands with some of its services having lost their relevance. To deal with the situation, the organization decided to conduct regional and, in some instances, countywide needs assessments via community group forums (town meetings). It sought advice on how these should be facilitated and what types of individuals would be best to lead them. The organization was leaning toward internal regional and local personnel to reduce costs. It asked a specialist in needs assessment to review its proposed approach. The advice was that this would not be a reasonable course to follow and it would be more beneficial to have a smaller number of sessions led by external individuals with the assistance and guidance of internal agency personnel.

The rationale behind this suggestion was that although the organization and its internal personnel had the best of intentions, bias could and would probably be evident in the results. No matter how much they try to not favor a particular viewpoint or vested interest, internal staff members might be unable to adopt the neutral stance necessary for facilitation. They carry historical baggage with them. In a subtle way, they could exude a slant on issues that may be obvious to participants at the start of group sessions or emerge as the forums get underway. The quality of results could be affected, with validity called into question.

In general, external facilitators will not be biased toward any specific position or program and serve as catalytic agents—that is, helping a group open up and uncover its perceptions, feelings, issues, and the like. The external facilitator may not have intimate knowledge of the situation and thus could benefit from the assistance of an internal expert or cofacilitator, but the tradeoff in neutrality is too great to make the case for being penny-wise by using internal staff to conduct the meetings.

Source: From *Needs Assessment: An Overview*, by J. W. Altschuld and D. D. Kumar, 2010, Thousand Oaks, CA: Sage. Used with permission.

As a general rule (not because that is the way we earn part of our bread), we posit that external facilitators are better. That would be particularly true in relation to having a breadth of experience and knowledge about methods. But there is a compromise that would be useful for most local needs assessments. Employ a consultant who can demonstrate prior success in the assessment process with success being defined as not only technical adequacy of the effort but additionally the empowerment of a cadre of committed individuals from the NAC who continue the assessment on their own initiative and with enthusiasm.

How is this accomplished? Here is what could be done. The external consultant should begin from the outset to build a basis for continuation as just described. Form subcommittees from the NAC and make sure that they have internal leadership rather than relying on the outsider. Emphasize as the whole enterprise moves forward that it should and in fact must become more of an internal activity. After all, a consultant simply will not be there to implement policies and new programs to resolve needs. Hopefully buy-in will have occurred and this transformation will not be particularly difficult. Another alternative would be to have an internal cofacilitator who, from the start as the work moves forward, slides into the main leadership role in a planned manner.

Even with emerging internal leadership or a leadership group, there will be aspects of the assessment where certain expertise will still be needed as the NAC proceeds, particularly to late Phase II or into Phase III activities. To that end, several days of the consultant's time might be contracted to review progress, to maintain contact, and to provide the skills and experience that might not be on hand in the organization. This continuing involvement recently happened with one of the authors, and after training personnel for needs assessment he will have a few extra days of service with them as they progress with further efforts. This would in our view be "pound wise." This may be a very good way of balancing out the assessment and help ensure an eventual positive result.

❖ HOW DO WE PUT THE DATA TOGETHER?

Returning to an earlier theme, there are three main decisions that will be made as we conclude Phase I. We can decide:

1. A need is not really there, and no further action is warranted;

2. A need is there, and we need to do a major assessment; or

3. A need is there, but we know enough now to turn to the action plan.

Synthesis of the data is obviously required with data sometimes lending themselves to being easily grouped and summarized. Unfortunately, a quick handling and early ending does not happen frequently. Why is difficulty often encountered in performing the seemingly easy task of pulling data together and drawing reasonable conclusions from them?

In thinking about needs there is the notion that they involve both values and "hard" facts. Data almost always come from mixed qualitative and quantitative methods, and those methods might even vary in their use with different stakeholder groups. Individual interviews might be conducted with high-ranking individuals, and focus group interviews might be conducted with service deliverers. The information would tend to be similar but not identical, as there generally are differences in the questions asked.

Another consideration is that in Phase I much of the data is from sources that already exist and are somewhat easy to find. As such they were probably not created for the needs expressly being explored at this time. We try to interpret and understand them in our context from what somebody else did for his or her own purposes and uses. We may be puzzled about criteria for entry and archiving and how the information was put into existing records, especially if it was excerpted from written commentary. We may not know all of the dimensions of creating the data set and what its subtle features are. We have to collate information that does or does not fit together and place it into findings that guide the decisions of the organization. Sample questions underlying the quest for meaning might be:

- How good were the data that were collected (are sources reliable, meaningful, and credible)?

- In terms of credibility, will the sources be perceived as believable to the organization and sections within it?

- Are the data appropriate for the concerns we are investigating?

- What has changed since the data were collected, and to what extent does it relate to our current situation (could it be too dated to be of much use to us)?

- Are there any gaps in the information, and are they serious enough to make us nervous about any recommendations being made (this nervousness might indicate that Phase II of needs assessment would be our logical decision choice)?

- Overall, how do we feel about the quality of what we have found or generated?

Is it any wonder that looking at needs can be a complicated activity even in Phase I? The hidden dilemma in the process is pulling together a composite view or synthesis. In this regard, Altschuld and Witkin (2000) described a major assessment that collected data using highly varied methods across a region of a country. Each method was well implemented, and the findings per method were carefully determined. While each had a separate report, a comprehensive one that integrated findings into decision-oriented mode was not available. That integration proved to be a difficult task.

Add to this the issue of weighting findings. How do we assess the quality of each source? Should some be seen as more important than others and hence receive a higher weighting? Should some sources be discredited, and if so, upon what basis should we take this action? Does "harder" quantitative data assume greater precedence than "softer" (supposedly) qualitative results, especially if we have an NAC that thinks this way as opposed to another quite uniquely constituted group? What happens if the outcome simply reflects the NAC's prejudices about the method? What do we do when the data from sources are good but provide not complementary information?

One way to operate here might be for the facilitator to discuss these issues with the NAC. Point out the strengths and weaknesses of the data and then engage committee members in thinking through how to proceed. Hopefully intelligent, thoughtful people will come to sensible and reasonable positions on what should be done. Your group will wrestle with such concerns and should be able to resolve them.

In Chapter 4 we provided several examples of summary tables that can be used in Phase I. There are many alternatives possible for these summaries, with the choices being left up to you and the NAC. Whatever you use, keep them as simple as possible and on point.

Once you have dealt with the data and summaries, which of the three decision choices given previously is to be recommended to the organization? How comfortable and confident is the NAC with what will be proposed? As the decision is made, be aware that resources in time and money saved at an early stage in needs assessment often pay dividends later, because these are resources that could be directed toward another part of the process or another activity—for example, in carrying out elements of a plan arising from the results of the endeavor.

If you decide on Option 3 (moving immediately to action planning), you gain efficiency—unless you do so without the critical information learned in a full and comprehensive effort. What Option 3 signifies is that we have sufficient knowledge to suggest a solution strategy for a major organizational problem or set of problems. Wow, what an outcome from Phase I exploration, and what an outcome without having to enter into the expensive Phase II! If there is a need, this is the best of all circumstances.

To cite advice given by a veteran needs assessor, Dr. Jefferson Eastmond (the father of one of the authors), a common pitfall in needs assessment studies is to expend far too many resources studying needs, coming out with too few resources to actually carry out an action plan. With a well-implemented Phase I and judicious use of the full study option (Phase II, should it be warranted), this overexpenditure of resources should be a rare rather than common occurrence.

Next steps, of course, depend on the choice selected. The most complicated one, conducting Phase II, is discussed at length in Book 3 of the KIT. If you move that way or to the other decision choice, rest assured that you have taken this action only after justifying why that is the best course to follow. It would seem that all has been said about the leftover pieces of Phase I, but there is one glaring, important omission that must be given serious attention for it could result in the failure of the whole endeavor and in many instances it has.

❖   HOW CAN ADEQUATE
COMMUNICATION BE MAINTAINED?

One of the authors attended a session of his statewide evaluation group in which a presenter made a rather striking observation. He noted that he had been involved in a very well-executed evaluation that from the standpoint of technical quality was a success but from the perspective of utilization would have to be judged a failure. This observation generalizes to the conduct of needs assessments.

What might have been factors contributing to underutilization? Consider the following possibilities:

- The methods may have been focused on one approach (quantitative or qualitative) and may not have been engaging or appealing enough to key decision makers.

- While much good information may have been located, it was not fully on-target with what was wanted or required for making decisions.

- Along with the above concern was the fact that the assessment just did not delve into the real concerns of the organization.

Collectively these points reflect the value of good communications throughout the entire process and particularly in Phase I as the activity begins. The facilitator should be cognizant of communication channels and use them at appropriate times to keep everyone in the loop. Consider what happened in the needs assessment described in Example 6.2.

Example 6.2

Lack of Communication and a Technically Successful but Nonetheless Failed Needs Assessment!

One of us conducted a training assessment for a specialized technical industry. It was commissioned by a nationwide consortium that provided training and coordinated various other services for the industry. The assessment would be characterized as perhaps being part of Phase I and part of Phase II.

(Continued)

(Continued)

About three quarters of the way through the effort, the management of the organization changed. The needs assessors did not see this as affecting much of anything since the new leadership was aware of the project and where it was going. In addition, good relations and support for the study were apparent from the involvement of most of the internal professional staff in regard to their help in interpreting data.

As things turned out, nothing could have been further from reality. Soon after the change at the top level, the final report was completed, and a summary was presented to the national advisory committee. Along with the results, possibilities for new directions and initiatives for organizational actions were made, all in accord with generally accepted ways of presenting suggestions.

At best the reception from the new administrators was lukewarm (an overstatement if there ever was one). We were thanked for our work, and the study essentially was tabled (read *killed*), and nothing ostensibly came from it. Parenthetically, several years later someone in the administration indicated that in retrospect the organization had missed capitalizing on the training needs uncovered in the assessment.

So why did this fail? Certainly, the new leaders had some reservations about the assessment and did not feel positive about it. There is no denying that. On the other hand, the assessors should have recognized that meeting and interacting with the new group was imperative as they were completing their work. They had incorrectly assumed that the same values remained in place as when the project began. This misperception was a fatal flaw, and the experience underscores why communication is so critical in needs assessment.

Given that such occurrences take place, what should be done to maintain lines of communication between the assessment process and the rest of the organization? *First,* make sure that all work is dated, especially as given or presented to higher-ups and staff. This historical feature helps demonstrate how conclusions were arrived at and how the field was narrowed from many needs to a smaller, focused set that would demand careful perusal. In Example 6.2, the organization, the consortium, lost a few million dollars in training business over the next several years. The needs assessors could have done a better job of informing and guiding pertinent deliberations. But in the end, the management of an organization has the ultimate responsibility for making decisions about whether or not to resolve identified needs. In the example a major opportunity was lost in an expensive way.

Second, there is a strong need to keep all key parties involved to some degree in the needs assessment process. In current environments this can easily be done by electronic means if people conscientiously read their e-mail. Newsletters and short updates will go a long way toward preventing any disconnects. These messages can be used not only to inform but also to increase interest in the endeavor.

As an illustration, let's say that in Phase I the NAC has found a very interesting set of articles about some aspects of the needs area. Going a little further it may be suspected that not many staff members are aware of or understand trends that may be affecting or eventually will affect the organization.

Why not take advantage of these facts by summarizing what the resources are saying in little notes to the organization? Perhaps a catchy title like "I'll bet you don't know" to pique imagination and interest would be useful. Or if the initial Phase I work had uncovered some little-known items, why not initiate a contest with a small prize (an inexpensive gift certificate for lunch at a nearby restaurant) for the staff member who comes closest to guessing the real number? This may sound a bit "gimmicky," but it makes the assessment more fun and creates more of an across-the-organization sense of ownership.

Third, it is a necessity that the decision makers be routinely informed of progress and even sounded out as to what their perceptions are about the progress to date. The eventual saving of time by communicating and when to communicate are two things to be thought about as the NAC interacts with individuals and across levels in the organization.

Administrators and staff are busy people; their time is a precious commodity. So make sure that all written communications are direct and to the point, and if further information is required, append it, but don't clutter any summaries that are distributed. The same would be true of any short meetings that are provided for presenting findings and progress. Make sure that some part of these sessions allows for comments and discussion of what is happening in the assessment. That input will help the effort and enhance the ownership of the enterprise. Such involvement is perceived to make the assessment better and flow more smoothly.

"Timing" is another dimension of communication. Obviously one point in the process would be when the needs assessment has been completed and findings and conclusions have been developed. When it is basically done and recommendations are at hand, invite input from staff and administrators, and if there are other alternatives or explanations coming from them, include those points in the final report. Other times for communications would be at major junctures in the process (some thought-provoking findings have been found) or when the facilitator and the NAC sense that it would be good for general information and there is enough to report. Sound out members of the NAC as to what might be propitious moments to do so. Ask them what they feel would be the best or most useful information for this purpose.

❖ SOME FINAL THOUGHTS ABOUT PHASE I

Phase I activities set the tone for the full implementation of an assessment and provide the basis for action (or inaction!). Many activities, steps, and procedures have been suggested and explained in varying levels of depth. If you have responsibility for the process, the task can seem overwhelming, especially in the case of a large and comprehensive study. The way to think about what is provided here and in other sources in the KIT (or elsewhere) is as a guide to the assessment, not a cast-in-stone formulaic approach. It is offered in more stoic terms: Use these steps, but your own judgment will keep you well grounded.

The NAC and its facilitator cannot do everything described in the text—there would not be enough time, money, human resources, spirit, and morale to try all procedures and specialized approaches, at least in a single study. The local situation, the nature of the players, political forces in play, organizational gestalt, and so many other variables determine and shape what should be done and what would be most efficacious. While needs assessments are similar in general structure, the devil lies in the minutiae of various local scenarios. What would be best is to review what is available in procedures and guidance, to select what is apropos, and finally to tailor and adopt it as the NAC sees fit.

The process of investigating needs can be very complex, complicated, and involved. It is critical to have a mechanism for tracking and documenting what steps have been taken and what has resulted from them. Following this prescription not only aids the evaluation of the needs assessment by having a running record of what happened for later use; it also helps in apportioning time efficiently and wisely. Groups can get sidetracked, retrace old ground ad infinitum, and, if they are not well focused, become bored with the entire endeavor with much of their effort being wasted. This is not a good outcome, and beyond some normal duplication, it should be avoided.

In this vein, remember to keep very good minutes of what transpires at NAC meetings and as stressed date all major products, especially tables and summaries generated by the group. This helps a group stay on task. A database with dated entries like this will be very useful in assessment work, and its importance cannot be overemphasized.

Chapter 1 in this book began with the idea of needs assessment being like a journey or an adventure. We truly believe that is exactly what it is about, and like all journeys it has obstacles and snags but also scenic vistas to be enjoyed and savored. To that end we again wish *bon voyage* and *bonne chance*.

❖ A LAST PIECE OF UNFINISHED BUSINESS: OUR RUNNING EXAMPLE

Let's look at the running example in regard to a few key elements emphasized in the chapter and book. Note that the needs assessment has been completed, so there is some reconstructed logic or retrospective recall in this analysis.

How much time was allotted? In this case, the plan called for completion of all elements of the study in one semester (5 months). In actual fact the final compilation and editing took half of another semester (3 months). This frequently happens. It just takes more time to implement the work, and writing it up is a fairly complicated and in-depth exercise. This latter observation is often overlooked or not well understood, and that is particularly true in this kind of work. Remember that an assessment might move into Phases II and III (resources would be required) and the ultimate results may lead to serious organizational change. Reports have to be drafted and written carefully.

In virtually every needs assessment with which we have been associated, we seem to have consistently underestimated what that final report would entail in terms of writing. Be alert to this possibility in your local setting. It might be wise to have a few insiders review the report and/or what might be highlighted in an oral presentation to decision makers. Their insights will be helpful as to how arguments have been framed, what has been cited, and many other pernicious yet important details.

Who should lead the group? One faculty member with previous experience conducting needs assessments, three of them for this department (1978, 1990, 2000), made the choice direct and easy. The advantages of credibility, insider knowledge, and costs were clear; the disadvantages were potentially "stepping on other faculty members' toes" and a short timeline, knowing that a sabbatical year for the individual was fast approaching (2 months after completion). Other disadvantages that could operate in a subtle manner in assessments (although perhaps not in this instance) are an internal, insider bias to the effort and some reluctance to open up about problems when the facilitator comes from the staff. There are under-the-surface decisions made in assessments, and there always will be. They are neither good nor bad, but they will be encountered and should be approached consciously and thoughtfully.

How did we put the data together? This effort used the data gathering and analysis efforts of two graduate-level classes taught during the same semester, one on campus and one taught face-to-face at another campus, 45 miles away. The data were compiled by student committees working independently, and the final report was assembled by one lead editor, a graduate student on campus. This was done both as a hands-on experience for students and as a way to reduce expenses. While there were some cons to doing this (there was less experience on the part of the students; their writing skills may not have been as strong), there definitely were pros. To a great degree, the students were apart from faculty and could be somewhat to much more objective. Again it is just one of those tradeoffs made in this type of work.

How was adequate communication maintained? Having a weekly session with both classes was of immense value. Periodic meetings with the NAC, back on campus, were anticipated, but due to demands upon both faculty and graduate student time, scheduling these meetings was difficult (and sometimes postponed). The NAC worked in more of an advisory role than as "worker bees." Having an administrator (department head) with an "open-door policy" (easily accessible when needed), as well as having excellent rapport between the facilitator and the department head, was a big plus. If the activity had not benefitted from this feature, it would have been necessary to establish communication channels and use them with some regularity. Keep in mind as mentioned earlier a technically good assessment will have greater likelihood of failure with inadequate communication being a major contributor to that outcome.

Key elements that stand out in retrospect are (a) having had some lead time before starting on this study (2 months) was important to put all the elements in place; (b) being able to harness students to carry out a lot of the elements of the plan—instrument design, data collection, analysis, and reporting—given limited monetary resources made for both a strong effort and an excellent learning experience; and (c) good rapport between researchers and administrators, plus a high level of collegiality among faculty, was important. The study is available on the Web at http://itls.usu.edu/files/Executive%20Summary2004.pdf. In this regard also see DeMars et al. (2004b).

Highlights of the Chapter

1. The basic premise of Chapter 6 was that there are some leftover issues to bringing a needs assessment to life, some of which may have come up before but now require more extensive attention.

2. Four main issues were examined: time for the assessment, who should lead it (the delicate balance of external leadership as compared to a more internal stance), pulling data and information together for Phase I decisions and why that proves to be difficult, and the essential nature of communication and how it can make or break the process.

3. There is no formula or set of rules for Phase I that we propose or offer; there is only guidance for what is hoped to be a good experience for the organization, the NAC, and the facilitator of the process.

4. The last highlight was that in an honest manner we tried to deconstruct the illustrative case that had been imbedded in the chapters. In some ways, it was not an ideal one, but it comes from the crucible of the real world and shows the compromises that so regularly disappear from formal reports and documents. As you do needs assessments, money will be tighter than is desirable and necessary for the job, and you will seek shortcuts and ways to get data and information that are as useful as possible within budget. We hope that our frank appraisal of what we did will help you be creative in your local context.

References

Altschuld, J. W. (2003, summer). *Workshop for Korean educators.* School of Educational Policy and Leadership, The Ohio State University–Columbus.

Altschuld, J. W., & Kumar, D. D. (2010). *Needs assessment: An overview.* Thousand Oaks, CA: Sage.

Altschuld, J. W., & Lepicki, T. (2007). *Needs assessment workshop.* Presentation for the California Department of Aging, Los Angeles.

Altschuld, J. W., & Lepicki, T. L. (in press). Needs assessment in human performance interventions. In R. Watkins & D. Leigh (Eds.), *The handbook for the selection and implementation of human performance interventions* (Chapter 2). San Francisco: Jossey-Bass.

Altschuld, J. W., & Thomas, P. T. (in press). Evaluating when the sponsor shifts priorities: An example from a business and industry setting. In J. Morrell (Ed.), *Unintended consequences case book.* New York: Guilford.

Altschuld, J. W., & Witkin, B. R. (2000). *From needs assessment to action: Transforming needs into solution strategies.* Thousand Oaks, CA: Sage.

American Evaluation Association (2009). *Guiding principles for evaluators.* At http://www.eval.org/Publications/GuidingPrinciples.asp, accessed 1 October 2009.

Brewer, E., Eastmond, J. N., Jr., & Geertsen, R. (2003). Considerations for assessing ethical issues. In M. A. Fitzgerald, M. Orey, and M. M. Branch (Eds.), *Educational media and technology yearbook 2003* (Vol. 28, pp. 67–76). Westport, CT: Libraries Unlimited.

Cameron, K. S., & Quinn, R. E. (2006). *Diagnosing and changing organizational culture, based upon the competing values framework.* San Francisco: Jossey-Bass.

Chiasera, J. M. (2005). *Examination of the determinants of overweight and diabetes mellitus in U.S. children.* Unpublished doctoral dissertation, The Ohio State University–Columbus.

DeMars, S., Mason, M. D., Gomez, J., Bell, C., Parker, P. P., Henson, S., et al. (2004a). *Final Report of the Needs Assessment for the USU IT Department, 2004.* Logan, UT: Department of Instructional Technology, Utah State University. (At http://itls.usu.edu/files/Final%20Report%202004. pdf, accessed 1 October 2009).

DeMars, S., Mason, M. D., Gomez, J., Bell, C., Parker, P. P., Henson, S., et al. (2004b). *Final Report of the Needs Assessment for the USU IT Department, 2004.* Logan, UT: Department of Instructional Technology, Utah State University. (At http://itls.usu.edu/files/Executive%20 Summary 2004.pdf, accessed 1 October 2009).

Eastmond, J. N., Jr., Witkin, B. R., & Burnham, B. (1987). How to limit a needs assessment. In *How to evaluate educational programs* (pp. 1–4). Capitol Publications.

Eyre, R. M. (1974). *The discovery of joy* (pp. 91–119). Salt Lake City, UT: Bookcraft.

Fetterman, D. (1997). *Ethnography step by step* (2nd ed.). Thousand Oaks, CA: Sage.

Fiorentine, R. (1993). Beyond equity in the delivery of alcohol and drug abuse treatment services. *Journal of Drug Issues, 23*(4), 559–577.

Hites, L. (2006). *Needs assessment perspectives from Tulane: What happened after Hurricane Katrina?* Panel presentation at the annual conference of the American Evaluation Association, Portland, OR.

Hung, H.-L., Altschuld, J. W., & Lee, Y.-F. (2008). Methodological and conceptual issues confronting a cross-country Delphi study of educational program evaluation. *Evaluation and Program Planning, 31,* 191–198.

Kenny, D. R. (2004). How to solve campus parking problems without adding more parking. *Chronicle of Higher Education, 50*(29), B22. Retrieved from http://chronicle.com/weekly/v50i2029b02201.html

Kumar, D. D., & Altschuld, J. W. (1999). Evaluation of an interactive media in science education. *Journal of Science Education and Technology, 8*(1), 55–65.

Lauffer, A. (1982). *Assessment tools: For practitioners, managers, and trainers.* Beverly Hills, CA: Sage.

National Science Foundation (NSF). (2002). *The cultural context of educational evaluation: A Native American perspective.* Arlington, VA: NSF Directorate for Education and Human Resources, Division of Research, Evaluation and Communication.

Rothwell, W. J., Hohne, C. K., & King, S. B. (2007). *Human performance improvement: Building practitioner competence* (pp. 11–113). New York: Elsevier.

Sanders, J. R. (1994). *Joint committee standards for educational evaluation: The program evaluation standards* (2nd Ed.) (pp. 87–92). Thousand Oaks, CA: Sage.

Scriven, M., & Roth, J. (1978). Needs assessment: Concept and practice. *New Directions for Program Evaluation* (AERA Monograph 1, pp. 39–83). Chicago: Rand McNally.

Scriven, M., & Roth, J. (1990). Needs assessment: Concepts and practice. Reprint in *Evaluation Practice, 11*(2), 135–144.

Stevahn, L., & King, J. (2010). *Needs assessment Phase III: Taking action for change.* Thousand Oaks, CA: Sage.

Thompson-Robinson, M., Hopson, R., & SenGupta, S. (2004, summer). In search of cultural competence in evaluation: Toward principles and practices. *New Directions for Evaluation, 102.*

Watkins, R., & Guerra, I. (2002). How do you determine whether assessment or evaluation is required? *ASTD T&D Sourcebook,* pp. 131–139.

Webb, E. J., Campbell, D. T., Schwartz, R. D., & Sechrest, L. (1969). *Unobtrusive measures: Nonreactive research in the social sciences.* Chicago: Rand McNally.

White, J. L., & Altschuld, J. W. (2009). *Issues and opportunities in consortium evaluations: Cross-sites, levels, and groups.* Paper presentation at the annual conference of the American Evaluation Association, Orlando, FL.

White, J. L., Altschuld, J. W., & Lee, Y.-F. (2008). Evaluating minority retention programs: Problems encountered and lessons learned from the Ohio Science and Engineering Alliance. *Evaluation and Program Planning, 31*(3), 277–283.

Witkin, B. R. (1984). *Assessing needs in educational and social programs: Using information to make decisions, set priorities, and allocate resources.* San Francisco: Jossey-Bass.

Witkin, B. R., & Altschuld, J. W. (1995). *Planning and conducting needs assessments: A practical guide.* Thousand Oaks, CA: Sage.

Witkin, B. R., & Eastmond, J. N., Jr. (1988). Bringing focus to the needs assessment study: The pre-assessment phase. *Educational Planning, 6*(4), 12–23.

Womack, J. P., & Jones, D. T. (2003). *Lean thinking.* New York: Simon & Schuster.

Index

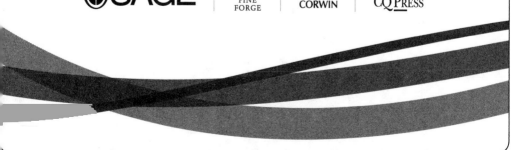